DAY TR

CW00505327

The Practical Guide to Start Building Your
Financial Freedom

(A Detailed and Practical Guide to Quickly Start to
Make a Profit)

Adam Lott

Published by Martin Debroh

Adam Lott

All Rights Reserved

ISBN 978-1-77485-083-1

Legal & Disclaimer

The information contained in this book is not designed to replace or take the place of any form of medicine or professional medical advice. The information in this book has been provided for educational and entertainment purposes only.

The information contained in this book has been compiled from sources deemed reliable, and it is accurate to the best of the Author's knowledge; however, the Author cannot guarantee its accuracy and validity and cannot be held liable for any errors or omissions. Changes are periodically made to this book. You must consult your doctor or get professional medical advice before using any of the suggested remedies, techniques, or information in this book.

Table of Contents

Introduction

What's the easiest way to make a million dollars in close to no time at all? That's a trick question, there is no easy way! However, there are some methods that are better suited to making a ton of money than others. It's no secret that the rich have always viewed the financial markets as being one of the key drivers of their wealth. Whatever their primary businesses may be, it is hard to find a single wealthy person who does not have some form of investment in the markets.

The beauty of the financial markets is that there are many ways for you to participate. You can buy and hold for the long run or you can buy something you like and sell it immediately. You can also sell first and buy back later. You can speculate on the basis of the monetary policy of some country and purchase stocks or currencies according to what your projections dictate. There really is no end to the number of ways in which the financial markets allow you to make money.

The flip side is that it is just as easy to lose money. If you can make money buying stocks you're equally likely to lose money speculating in FX (Forex, that is, currency pairs.) Learning how to trade is a key skill you must master if you wish to not only survive in the markets but also thrive. It seems odd to say this but it is the large number of options available that causes a lot of prospective traders to stumble.

Truth be told, it isn't just beginner traders but also experienced ones who bite the dust. Trading is not an easy endeavor and requires a lot of preparation. The question to ask yourself at this point is: How much are you willing to put into this? There are huge rewards on offer but to expect them to fall into your lap is wishful thinking. You're going to have to work for it and along the way, you'll have to face some of your biggest fears.

Risk and Reward

The willingness to work is one thing but knowing how to work and what to do is another. This is where this book is going to help you. This is not a book which is going to give you a few indicators and tell you to go copy paste them onto a price chart. Truth be told, such methods don't really work anymore.

You need to be a lot smarter than the average trader in the market because that is who you're competing against. This doesn't mean all indicators are useless. It's just that you need to learn how to use them. The old ways of using indicators will only lose you money because everyone is using them the same way. This book will introduce you to some evergreen strategies involving indicators and price charts that will make you money from day one.

Speaking of price charts, most traders have a deep fear of it. After all, it can be intimidating to stare at the right edge of the price chart and try to decide what to do next. There is no specific formula anyone can give you for every situation in the market. Instead of looking to memorize a few patterns here and there or a few geometric shapes, you will need to learn how to play the odds.

At its heart, trading is all about playing the odds and understanding probabilities. What does that mean, exactly? In it's most basic form, trading success is all about following some very basic arithmetic. That's right! You don't need to learn differential calculus to understand the markets.

You're free to do so, of course, but do you really want to over complicate what is essentially a simple process? Trading might be difficult but it is certainly not complex. This is what this book is going to teach you. There is something that cannot be taught to you by anybody else though. This is something that only you can address and figure out. I'm referring to yourself or to be more specific: What your mindset is like.

Trading and You

Trading success requires hard work and great risk management. Risk management has two portions to it: First, there is the mathematical portion where you'll need to understand the odds of your system and understand when to deploy your strategies. The second sounds simple but is actually one of the hardest things you'll ever do.

It deals with figuring yourself out. What moves you and what are your beliefs and fears about money? When dealing with uncertainty, how do you respond? These are just some of the questions about yourself you will have to explore and the mindset and risk management section of this book is going to help you do exactly that.

Believe it or not, the technical portion of trading which involves finding entries and timing exits is the easy bit. You think this is tough because you haven't had good instruction as yet in this regard. Exploring yourself and fixing your mindset is a task that sounds easy but is actually difficult. Few prospective traders follow through with actions in this regard.

One of the best ways to hold yourself accountable is to create a trading plan. To be more specific, you need to create a business plan for your trading because that's what it really is. You're not looking at indulging in a hobby when it comes to trading. Either you run it as a business or you'll end up donating your money to the market (which will have no hesitation in accepting it.)

Once you master the tools provided in this book, your trading will become unstoppable. The key for you is to put in the work and follow through on your desire to become a great trader. Whether you're an absolute beginner or whether you're looking for a new strategy to boost your trading, you've come to the right place.

So having said all that, let's get started and take a look at the one thing that is central to trading: The Market.

Chapter 1: What Is Online Trading?

What is Online Trading

Online trading is only buying and selling financial securities via an online trading platform. This online trading software is made available to traders, usually for free, by internet brokers. The internet brokers are accessible to anyone wishing to invest in the stock market and negotiate financial instruments on the markets.

Online trading is, therefore, about speculating in the financial markets, trying to take advantage of changes in asset prices to earn money between the time of purchase and resale, or conversely, because it is possible to sell a product that we do not own.

Online trading is a severe activity that must be understood as a profession and not a way to quickly earn a lot of money without risk and without knowing anything about it. Apart from that, it is true that online trading is accessible to all those who are ready to work hard and to get 100% involved in this activity where the psychological is a daily challenge.

Origin of Online Trading

Online trading has increased significantly since the 1990s, technological advances made in high-speed computing computers, at affordable prices, and to Internet connections

Internet: People are now using the Internet to invest and trade. The growth of the Internet is staggering thanks to its accessibility, as evidenced by global statistics.

Computers: Moore's Law states that the overall processing power of networks will double every two years, allowing the trader to quickly connect to the Internet and do his analysis on his computer.

Both of these trends have led to rapid growth in online trading and have made access to financial markets as unprecedented as ever. More people can trade online, and this trend seems to

increase exponentially. Especially since more than 1.7 billion people with a mobile phone remain excluded from the financial system, but not for long!

WHAT IS CFD TRADING?

CFD trading is the act of buying and selling one or more CFD products.

To better understand stock exchange CFDs and their importance to the particular trader, we will list the characteristics of a CFD.

Firstly, "CFD" comes from the English "Contract For Difference," which means " Contract for the difference. " It is a derivative product applicable almost to all financial products such as:

Stock indices

Forex

Raw materials

Explained most simply, the CFD makes it possible to speculate on the rise and fall of the value of a currency pair, an index, or even gold.

This type of trading online has become very popular since trading on CFD enhances the speculation to and fro of many financial products like commodities, stocks, or stock indices and especially with little money.

WHAT IS FOREX TRADING

Forex market is known as the foreign exchange market, where there are currencies for trading. The currency market simply signifies the respective values of money relative to each other.

Forex trading is the activity of investment of currency pairs like:

Euro Yen Japanese EUR JPY

Euro Dollar EUR USD

British Pound Dollar GBP USD

Dollar Yen Japanese USD JPY

Forex trading is prevalent.

This can be explained very simply in terms of its merits:

Strong Forex liquidity with significant volumes in the currency market

Real-time Forex trading (24 hours per day, five days per week)

It is a day and night market, allowing Forex traders around the world to trade the Forex courses of their choice. Significant liquidity means the ability to get in and out of the Forex market at any time! The euro and the US dollar are both at the top of the list of the most traded currencies!

In particular, the foreign exchange market has reduced fees, which makes it very accessible for a novice trader and has several features such as leverage, spread, and the size of the CFD contract.

A TRADER IS WHAT?

The profile of the trader can be defined under three distinct but complementary and indissociable categories:

The analyst, the trader, analyzes the context in which a particular instrument is located, using fundamental analysis and technical analysis. However, it is common to see specific traders use only one of these two analyzes.

The actual trader, who buys and sells instruments like CFDs to make gains, based on the difference between the buying and selling price of trading positions.

The risk manager, since the trader must first and foremost manage the risk, he takes on the markets to remain lucrative and continue his work.

You understand that a trader must be able to wear several hats to carry out his online trading activity in the best conditions. Still, a trader is first and foremost a financial market professional, knowing how it works and how to interpret and read trades — visible price fluctuations on the trading charts to profit from them.

Trading - What is DAY Trading

There are many ways to do online trading.

These different approaches are defined according to the trading period to which you are available and according to the trader's personality. We can thus distinguish:

DAY Trading

the Day Trading

Scalping or High-Frequency Trading

Trading is What - Participants

The most imperative players in the financial markets are:

The states

Other banks

The Hedge Funds

Investment Funds

Brokers

Professional Investors

Private Investors

As the Forex market is concerned, the participants with the most weight and impact on currency prices are undoubtedly the central banks. A central bank is the currency provider for the country in which it operates and is, therefore, the supply in this market. Its decisions have a significant impact on the price of currency pairs.

Small investors, like individual traders, have a very slight influence on the market, but this influence is evident because of their large numbers.

To understand the forex, we must know that the supply and demand of currencies are constantly changing, and we can see the movement of prices on a tick chart on the online trading platform, for example.

The other players in online trading are professional traders and private traders (or home traders). Both categories negotiate financial contracts through an online trading platform.

Professional traders are either Traders for their account or Traders on behalf of their clients.

Private traders are, in turn, traders on their behalf for the most part.

THE BASICS OF STOCK MARKET INVESTING FOR BEGINNERS

BASIC KNOWLEDGE OF A TRADER

What do you need to know to become a good trader?

Becoming a good trader is a learning process. A trader must have basic knowledge, supplemented with experience.

Basic knowledge includes:

Product knowledge :

Which product traded with? CFDs or Contracts for Difference are popular trading instruments and popular with novice and experienced traders. In section Trading with CFDs everything about this investment instrument.

Money management and risk management

Risk management or money management is crucial to succeeding as a trader. After all, his money is his working capital. How much risk do you take? Set how much leverage? Where to place the stop. With the answers to these questions, you protect profits and your trading capital, and you limit your losses.

Technical analysis helps the trader to make his investment decisions. What is the trend? Are you trading long or short? Which signals from which indicators apply? What do course patterns learn? A lot of information can be read from the signs. An interesting tool is the WHS Tech scan. WHS Techscan scan every evening for technical signals at almost all exhibitions.

Develop a trading strategy

A trader develops and tests a trading strategy or better: multiple trading strategies. What does a good plan have to meet? How to test a strategy? The section Developing strategies such as the MACD 1% strategy and the Triple Screen strategy shows based on various simple trading strategies on how a trader builds a plan and what the points for attention are.

Knowledge of the trading platform

A trader must have mastered his trading platform. Various types of orders allow targeted entry into the market. It is advisable to practice well on a demo platform. With a demo platform, you can develop and apply your strategies for free with real-time prices and thus gain experience.

Chapter 2: Why You Are Not Yet Permanently Successful On The Stock Market

Do You Know Why? I'll tell you directly:
1. Because you have the wrong knowledge about the market.
 2. Because you rely on technical Analysis.
 3. Because you have no advantage over the mass - ie no advantage over the other market participants.
 4. You trade the wrong market - Binary Options, Forex or CFD

One must be clear to you. You have to understand who moves the market. A Double Top, or Double Bottom Formation is nothing, because you do not see how many contracts are traded. You have to look behind the candles.

The main problem with binary options is that you do not have reasonable risk management. There you have no risk management, because your Win/Loss Ratio isALWAYS negative! Let's say you invest, for example, 100 € and with a return of85%, you get 85 € profit on an investment of ... 100 €. This is bad! No professional trader acts like that. One of the most important requirements for professional trading is the POSITIVE Win/Loss Ratio (At least 1: 1, better 1.5: 1, best 2: 1 and more)
 The second major problem with Binary options is that you have an expiration time
 - 60 seconds, 120 seconds, 240 seconds etc. That means you have no control over your "position".

In trading, it is important to be adaptable and to react to the current situation. No control over your position, bad Win/Loss Ratio... and there are even more disadvantages.

Third problem: With the binary options you always act against the broker! Here, if you win, the broker loses. In addition, it happens very often that the broker manipulated the course! Sometimes a price fluctuation of only 1 micro-lot may be the reason you lose (micro-lot is the smallest position size you trade in Forex and CFD) and this is precisely the price fluctuation that can arise from a manipulation of the broker! But no one tells you this...

The broker just wants to win new customers - because the very customers are the lifeblood of every Binary Options, CFD and Forex Broker. The ugly truth...

Forex and CFD have one more problem - spread. In addition to potential price manipulation, it is also possible that the spread may be deliberately widened which in many cases can be the reason for the stop-out - this is a "strategy" the broker uses to earn his money. That's why I've already mentioned that neither Binary Options, nor Forex or CFD are transparent markets. Trading on CFD and Forex is also not on the stock market, as most people think, but through the broker. The prices in CFD and Forex are determined by the so-called "market maker" - such prices differ from the reference exchange.

No institutional trader or professional private trader uses Binary Options, CFD or Forex. As a private investor you have only disadvantages in such a market - No transparency and price manipulation. One of the biggest drawbacks, as mentioned before, is that you have no advantage over other market participants.

You are missing the most important piece of information - it stays hidden and most traders who use technical analysis, do not have this information.

Only the institutional traders and the private, professional traders see behind the scenes, behind the chart. And that is exactly the right way the only way that I will describe in great detail later on. The information, that will change your life.I will give you many, many practical examples, insider tips and instructions.

Chapter 3: How To Get Started

So, now that you understand what day trading is, you many have your interest peaked, and so you want to know how to get started.

A thing with day trading is that, while it seems easy and straightforward on the surface, it is a complicated and risky venture that will often need you to take your time to understand it, then be willing to put your time in it. Day trading will take your time, and thus, you need to be in a position to put in the hours.

That said, you will need to get a few things right if you want to get started.

Conduct Your Research

A thing you will notice when you get into day trading is that a number of the people in the field are seasoned. They are well-established and knowledgeable in the area. Thus, to make it in this field, you will need to do your due diligence.

Getting into day trading without understanding the market will mean only one thing – you will lose money. Take your time to understand the more in-depth details of the market you want to trade-in, and then, what assets exist.

Day traders also are in tune with events that result in the short-term movements of the market. So, you will also need to look into it. Many trading throughout the day will be affected by political scenarios, significant announcements, corporate earnings, and market expectations. So, this means that say there is political upheaval, then the stocks might go down as traders hold onto their assets as they maintain a wait-and-see approach. Understanding when heads will make major events or announcements will also be useful for you so that you can plan your day around the game, as well as look into the history of how the report affects the stock.

Put Aside Sufficient Capital

As we said in chapter one, day trading will need you to be willing to put aside your time and capital if you are going to realize any profits. This money that you set aside for your day trading venture is the risk capital.

One of the things about day trading is that day traders often deal with large volumes of trade. So, they do not venture into just one or two ventures. They will venture into as many as thirty deals. That is a lot of money to put into it.

Thus, because of the compressed profits of day trading, to see the gains accumulate to substantial benefits, you will need to risk a large amount of money so that you can capitalize on the day's price movements. Make use of a margin account, as you will find it useful. A margin account is an account that is run by a broker who then uses it to lend to the trader so that they can purchase assets. This account comes in handy later when you want to risk more into the trade but may have limited risk capital.

In the U.S., to set up a day trading venture, you will need anything between USD 25,000 to 30,000. However, you can find this information from your stock market trader in your area. Create a rapport with them before you set aside your capital.

Have a Strategy

To invest in day trade is to be a strategist. Through the countless hours you will spend doing your market and technical analysis, and you will find that having a plan will be critical in how you will execute your plan to get into the trade and hold then close at the right time. You will use these strategies repeatedly until you then refine them, and they begin to help you make profits.

So, to create a strategy, you will need to ask yourself a few questions.

How do I get started? And how will I close, both after winning or losing?

How much am I willing to risk, and for how long will I risk it? What trade will I want my money into? What position would I take in the deal?

How many shares of stocks or currency?

Once you decide all this, then you begin the second phase.

How volatile is the trade-in day-to-day exchanges? What are the odds of making a profit from these movements?

While these questions are those that you will ask yourself before you start, once you get started, you will then need to implement them time and time again so that you can refine them and see which methods work better for you and how they work.

This plan will also help in devising whether you will develop a contrarian approach, which involves you bucking the trend and focusing your attention on unpopular strategies or whether you follow the pattern.

Both approaches have their time and place and are dependent on the market and stocks. It is also critical that you familiarize yourself with the knowledge that being contrarian is not just about going against the trend just for the sake of it. Neither is following the pattern just for the purpose of it. To use either of these approaches, you will conduct your research into both, find out how and where and when you will use them.

However, as a beginner, you may need to take your time and speculate on following the trend as you gain experience and learn of how you may make reasonable speculations on unpopular stocks and markets.

Know Your Limits

When you start day trading, you know that you need to sell before the market closes for the day. So, when you miss selling at the close of the market, you then will incur heavy losses as the change in prices in a day in the stock market is highly volatile.

So, set achievable targets when you begin to trade and do not exceed these targets. If you start buying the find that your profits begin to grow, rather than pour more money into the trade just because you have more, make plans on how you will increase your limits. You do not want to get into a scenario where you get huge returns but then find yourself incurring huge losses because you do not put in place goals that keep you in check.

You will then need to be very disciplined, sticking to your original plan and not getting swayed by what occurs in between the trade. As the traders will often say, you need to plan your trade, then trade the plan.

Find a Broker

You will conduct your trading in an investment platform, so choosing a broker will be a significant step in helping you make wise choices when you begin to trade. The broker will be in charge of your account, and you will then execute your trade through their platforms.

To choose your broker, consider a few things;

What are you trading? Different brokers will serve you depending on their area of specialization. So, if you want to go into forex, then find a forex broker. If you're going to go into stocks, find a stockbroker.

Check out the commission and brokerage fee. These charges will often eat into your money. So, it is necessary that you find a broker that charges reasonable prices, lest you find that you are spending a lot more of your money on these charges than on the actual trade.

Talk to other traders in your field to find out what they use and would recommend. Recommendations are a great way to find out which broker to trust with your account. Reputation is critical in the financial market, so talk to other traders, read about the broker, examine them comprehensively, and look at their history.

Are they up to the task? Day trading is quick, and thus, you will need a broker that is up to the task. So, find out if your broker can run multiple deals and execute numerous orders. Can they handle enormous volumes of trades? Do they give real-time feedback? Do they offer market news updates regularly? A day trade is to be in the know. Thus, you will need a broker that will keep you in the loop time and time again.

Always consider customer service. What do the brokers offer to their customers after-service? How do they deal with complaints? How do they treat their customers when they come to them with a problem? The understanding of their customer service will be essential so that you will know how they will deal with your situation when you complain to them.

Day trading, as we see above, is a purchase and sale of securities within a very volatile and fluctuating environment of a day. Therefore, while you will find significant profits in it when you make the

32

right moves and trade with gains, you will need to take your time to plan and execute it. Remember, you need to complete the deal within a day. Thus, you will need to continually monitor the market, aware of the small changes taking place. You will also be making different trades, tens of them; thus, you will need to have the time to trade it.

So, planning is what will get you to reap the benefits of day trading.

Chapter 4: What Is Day Trading?

Day trading is the buying and selling of securities in one single trading day. This can occur in any type of marketplace that you choose but it is most common in the stock market and in the forex market.

Day trading is very fast paced. You will purchase a stock, bond, option or other security at some point during the day. Then, sometime during the same day, you will sell the security. If you watched the market properly and the trade goes well, you will make a profit from that sale. If you made a mistake with your calculations, you will lose money.

Day trading is a strategy of trading financial securities, such as stocks and currencies, where positions are taken and closed within the same day. Also called short trading, it involves buying a financial security and selling them before the trading day closes.

How short can day trading last? It can be as short as buying and selling in a few minutes, or even seconds! The point is to end the trading day with a square position, i.e., neither long nor short on any financial security.

It doesn't matter how many trades you do during the day. You can trade just once a day or 10 times a day...it doesn't matter. The defining characteristic of day trading is ending the day with a square position.

Day trading can take place in any market, but the most common ones are the stock market and foreign exchange or forex markets.

When you start day trading, you'll need to start looking at financial securities from a different vantage point. For example, if you're used to swing trading or a buy-and-hold approach to stock market investing, you'll need to look at stocks differently when you day trade if you want to profit from it.

Instead of having a longer-term perspective on stocks, you'll need to reorient it to a very short-term one. In particular, you should shift your focus from a company's possible growth over the long term to its possible immediate price actions during the day.

Another area where you'll need to reorient your thinking are gains. Instead of looking at substantial gains, e.g., 10% or more, you'll need to scale down. Given the short time frame, you may have to make do with gains as low as 1% to 2%. This is because day trading involves trading at a higher frequency but with smaller gains, which accumulate over time.

You do not want to let your trade go on to the next day. This requires a different type of strategy than you will use with day trading. Mixing strategies during the same trade just to avoid a loss will actually make things worse. It is better to cut your losses with that trade and move on, closing out the trade before the end of the day.

With day trading, you are not going to make a ton of money off each trade. In fact, if you make a few dollars with each trade, you are doing a good job. The point here is to do a lot of little trades, taking advantage of the temporary ups and downs of the market. A lot of little profits can add up to a good payday when the process is done.

The potential profit that you can make from day traded is often misunderstood on Wall Street. There are many internet scams that like to take on this confusion and capitalize on it making a ton of money by promising large returns in a short period of time. On the other side, the media continues to promote this trading method as a get rich quick scheme.

To determine whether you will be successful depends on a few important factors. Mainly, if you jump into the day trading game without enough knowledge about the market and how this trading method works, you will probably fail. But there are many day traders who are able to make a successful living from day trading. These individuals know about the market, have a good strategy in place, and can work with the market, despite the risks.

Day trading can be difficult. There are many professional financial advisors and money managers who worry about the risk of day trading and will shy away from it. They worry that in many cases, the reward is not going to justify all the risk that you take with day trading. It is possible to make a profit in this method but you have to really know the market and you must have the time to fully watch the market at all times while completing your trade. Even those who do well in day trading will admit that the success rate with this method is often lower than the other methods of stock market trading.

Day trading isn't just restricted to stocks. You can day trade currencies, you can day trade commodities as well as options. Day trading involves more of a set of practices that you stick to.

Day trading is the very definition of short term trading. It's all about the short term. In fact, your trading horizon is restricted to one day. This means that you open a position and you close it strictly within one day's trading hours. You engage in it daily, you focus on one or more stocks or one or more commodities or currency pairings or options.

It's important to keep in mind that all your positions are liquidated by the end of the day. Whether you make money or not, you are out of your position by the end of the day. That is the key definition of day trading.

How Day Trading Decisions Are Made

A day trader's decision whether to enter a stock or exit a stock all boils down to the probable movement of the pricing of the stock within the trading period. The trading period can be as short as 5 minutes or less or it can be the whole day. Whatever the case may be, it doesn't exceed the whole day.

Day traders make money off volatility. They do not make as much money when the stock is trading sideways for a long time and gradually slopes up. A stock might gain value 10% over the course of a year, but that stock, for all intents and purposes, is off limits to a day trader because the volatility isn't there. They would rather trade a stock that bounces 15% up and down, every single day. That stock has enough internal volatility on a day to day basis for day traders to make quite a bit of money.

What Benefit Do Day Traders Offer to the Market?

In terms of economic benefits, how does day trading benefit stock trading as a whole? Well, if anything, day traders provide liquidity to the stock market. They offer a ready base of buyers and sellers of stock. This provides the necessary movement of a stock's price that may encourage other traders to look at either the short term or long-term value and prospects of the stock. In other words, by providing action on a strictly short-term basis, day traders tend to shine a light on the overall attractiveness of a stock.

Keep in mind this is quite ironic because day traders, as a rule, do not look at the fundamentals of a stock. They don't look at the price/earnings ratio or P/E. They don't look at long term value, they don't look at industry positioning. They couldn't care less about any of that. Instead, they focus more on momentum, share movement, share volume and price velocity going either up or down.

How Day Trading Works

Once you start day trading, you can use a myriad number of techniques and methods to execute trades. For example, you can choose to trade based solely on your "gut feeling" or you can go to the other extreme of relying entirely on mathematical models that optimize trading success through elaborate automated trading systems.

Regardless of the method, you can have limitless day-trading profit potential once you master day trading. Here are some of the strategies many expert day traders use profitably.

One is what's called "trading the news", which is one of the most popular day trading strategies since time immemorial. As you may have already gleaned from the name, it involves acting upon any press-released information such as economic data, interest rates, and corporate earnings.

Another popular day trading strategy is called "fading the gap at the open". This one's applicable on trading days when a security's price opens with a gap, i.e., below the previous day's lowest price or above the previous day's highest price.

"Fading the gap at the open" means taking an opposite position from the gap's direction. If the price opens with a downward gap, i.e., below the previous day's lowest price, you buy the security. If the price opens with an upward gap, i.e., it opens higher than the previous day's highest price, you short or sell the security.

There was a time when the only people able to trade in financial markets were those working for trading houses, brokerages, and financial institutions. The rise of the internet, however, made things easier for individual traders to get in on the action. Day Trading, in particular, can be a very profitable career, as long as one goes about it in the right way.

However, it can be quite challenging for new traders, especially those who lack a good strategy. Furthermore, even the most experienced day traders hit rough patches occasionally. As stated earlier, Day Trading is the purchase and sale of an asset within a single trading day. It can happen in any marketplace, but it is more common in the stock and forex markets.

Day traders use short-term trading strategies and a high level of leverage to take advantage of small price movements in highly liquid currencies or stocks. Experienced day traders have their finger on events that lead to short-term price movements, such as the news, corporate earnings, economic statistics, and interest rates, which are subject to market psychology and market expectations.

When the market exceeds or fails to meet those expectations, it causes unexpected, significant moves that can benefit attuned day traders. However, venturing into this line of business is not a decision prospective day trader should take lightly. It is possible for day traders to make a comfortable living trading for a few hours each day.

However, for new traders, this kind of success takes time. Think like several months or more than a year. For most day traders, the first year is quite tough. It is full of numerous wins and losses, which can stretch anyone's nerves to the limit.

Therefore, a day trader's first realistic goal should be to hold on to his/her trading capital.

Volatility is the name of the game when it comes to Day Trading. Traders rely on a market or stock's fluctuations to make money. They prefer stocks that bounce around several times a day, but do not care about the reason for those price fluctuations. Day traders will also go for stocks with high liquidity, which will allow them to enter and exit positions without affecting the price of the stock.

Day traders might short sell a stock if its price is decreasing or purchase if it is increasing. Actually, they might trade it several times in a day, purchasing it and short-selling it a number of times, based on the changing market sentiment. In spite of the trading strategy used, their wish is for the stock price to move.

Day Trading, however, is tricky for two main reasons. Firstly, day traders often compete with professionals, and secondly, they tend to have psychological biases that complicate the trading process.

Professional day traders understand the traps and tricks of this form of trading. In addition, they leverage personal connections, trading data subscriptions, and state-of-the-art technology to succeed. However, they still make losing trades. Some of these professionals are high-frequency traders whose aim is to skim pennies off every trade.

The Day Trading field is a crowded playground, which is why professional day traders love the participation of inexperienced traders. Essentially, it helps them make more money. In addition, retail traders tend to hold on to losing trades too long and sell winning trades too early.

Due to the urge to close a profitable trade to make some money, retail investors sort of pick the flowers and water the weeds. In other words, they have a strong aversion to making even a small loss. This tends to tie their hands behind their backs when it comes to purchasing a declining asset. This is due to the fear that it might decline further.

Chapter 5: Starting A Day Trading

Business

Some people, especially the beginners, rush into day trading business only to rush out. They ventured into this line of business only for the sole purpose of making money quickly without investing anything at all. Although, there's a lot of money to be made in the business if you don't keep your guards down. But engaging in it without fully understanding the rudiments, only to think you will start making money immediately is wrong. For every business, there are better days and there are days you'll get hurt. Learning to balance things is the key here. Professional and successful day traders go into day trading like it is their life. They give it all their attention without expecting any instant gratification.

UNIQUE TOOLS OF DAY TRADING

Day trading is online with little to no physical interaction. Day trading requires you to have access to basic internet connection, a computer, smartphones for backup internet, a phone to be able to reach your brokerage person etc. Some other very important tools for a successful day trader include; a direct access to a trusted brokerage, a real-time market data, and a trading-charting platform.

●Desktop computer or laptop: You cannot negotiate a fast and up-to-date computer for anything when it comes to day trading business. Most software you'll need to be running on your computers are very powerful. A higher memory is needed to be able to actively support these operations. Having two monitors is in fact okay but never compulsory.

●Day Trading Charting Software:

Brokers want their clients (day traders) to have some software, which will enable them to monitor trades on their computers. Financial charts problems are solved and explained by these software. Being able to find the best software for your trading needs and connecting them with your trading service is paramount for the overall success of your trading activities. Ninjatrader is a popular software used for trading and charting purposes.

●Telephone: Find a way to save your broker's number in case you want to contact them offline, without using mails.

●Effective internet connection: Day trading involves loading many websites and data daily. Having a very fast network is crucial so that you won't be found lagging sometimes when you urgently needed to access some very important information.

●Smartphones: Your phone mobile data plan can be used as an alternative internet connection when your computer internet is not connecting. Just connect your phone's Hotspot with your computer and you're good to go.

•Brokerage: You need a brokerage to help you through your trading solutions. Financial institutions such as banks provide brokerage services, only that their commission might be too high. There are many smaller but competent brokers out there that a day trader can choose from. What you need to do is to find a broker that allows you to use a specific trading software you will like to use. Day trading at different market levels may require you to use different brokers for each market.

•Market data: Day trading requires a constant source of financial data, especially from the market you're trading in. You will have access to timely data, only you have to tell your broker specifically which type of financial data you want. Some brokers won't charge you for these data but their commission will be high at the end of the day.

Now, let's take a look at some of the old and latest software used in the day trading market.

Trade Ideas: This is an automated system relying essentially on programmed Artificial intelligence to scan series of ideas needed for startup day traders. It searches for thousands of stock ideas, carries out background research about stocks, and gives users varied stock information that can enable them to make informed decisions. The pricing ranges between $1068 standard plan to $2268 premium plan. There's also a free subscription that comes with few features.

TradingView: This is a stock analysis software. It also enables you to view different price charts used to search for multiple assets such as cryptocurrency, bonds, commodities, futures etc. There's a basic subscription and there's a premium membership.

Benziga Pro: First surfaced in 2010. Gives users latest happenings in the financial markets. Searches for background data that takes you one-step ahead of latest financial findings.

eSignal: One of the oldest financial charting solutions. It links you directly to many brokerage firms.

TC2000: This presents users with charts that are easy to follow and relate with. It also provides you with premium analysis tools.

EquityFeed: Provides you with premium tools needed to give you an edge in the market. It has the ability to search for brokers online just for you.

FinVix Elite: Provide you with some premium charting tools and wonderful market news. Helps you identify investment opportunities.

DAY TRADING PATTERNS THAT WORKS

Every day you are presented with a mutiny of opportunities to choose between thousands of available trading opportunities. This is due to a wide range of factors influencing the day trading market. Day trading patterns enable you to decode multitude of options and motivations, including hope of gain and fear of loss, short-covering, stop-loss triggers, hedging, tax consequences etc.

Candlestick patterns help by giving you a vivid picture, and revealing to you trading signals and signs of future price movements. Whilst it is unarguable that you will need to exploit some technical analysis to succeed day trading with candlestick and other patterns, it is equally pertinent to reinstate that utilising them to your advantage is more of an art and should be imbibed. Here, we will talk about some popular day trading patterns, including breakouts and reversals. Your own is just to identify the best patterns to assist your trading style and methods.

Breakout – Occurs when the price clears a specified critical level on your chart. This level could by any number of things, from an advanced level to support, resistance or trend lines. A breakout is usually identified as a potential trading opportunity that occurs when the price of an asset moves above a resistance level or moves below a support level on incremental rate.

The first thing you should know in trading breakouts is how to identify current price trend patterns along with support and resistance levels so that you'll be able to plan possible entry and exit routes. Once you've taken action on a break out report, you must then determine when to cut your losses and assess the situation again if the breakout sputters. A breakout trader can enter a long position after the market's stock price breaks above resistance or enters a short position after the stock price breaks below support. Once the stock trades beyond the price barrier, volatility tends to increase and prices usually trend within the breakout's region. The reason breakouts are very important trading strategies is because they form the framework for future volatility increases, large price swings and, in many circumstances, noticeable price trends in the market. Breakouts typically dominate all types of market spaces. More often than not, the most noticeable price movements are one resulting from a channel breakouts and price pattern breakouts such as triangles, flags, or head and shoulders patterns. As volatility contracts during these time patterns, we will have expansion after prices move beyond the identified ranges. The graph below represents a triangle breakout curve.

Source: Cleveland Cliff

When trading breakouts, it is pertinent to consider the prevailing stock's support and resistance levels. The more times the stock price touches these areas, the more valid and profound the outcome.

Source: JC Penney

Reversal – This is just a change in direction of a price trend, which could be either positive or negative against the prevailing trend also, called a trend reversal. Certain indexes, such as moving average, oscillator, or channel, may help in identifying trends as well as understanding reversals. Reversals identify large price changes, wherever the trend changes direction. Small counter-moves against these trends are called pullbacks or consolidations. Reversals are often common in intraday trading and happen rather very fast, but they also occur across days, weeks, and years. Reversals occur on different time frames which are peculiar to different traders. An intraday reversal on a five-minute chart doesn't especially matter to a long-term investor who is on the lookout for a reversal on a daily or a weekly chart. Yet, the same five-minute is very important to a day trader. An uptrend - a series of higher swing highs and higher lows, snaps back into a downtrend by reversing to a series of lower highs and lower lows. A downtrend - a series of lower highs and lower lows, snaps back into an uptrend by reversing to a series of higher highs and higher lows.

The chart below indicates an uptrend moving with a channel, making a series of higher highs and higher lows. The price breaks out of the channel initially and below the trendline, indicating possible trend change. The price also makes a lower low by dropping below the prior low within the channel. This further validates the reversal to the downside.

Candlestick chart: the patterns are pretty straightforward to interpret. Also trading with candle patterns can help you attain that competitive edge over the rest of the traders in the market. There are about three most popular candlestick charts most commonly used. These include shooting star candlestick, doji and hammer candlestick. Candlesticks work by building patterns that can predict price direction once completed. A candlestick displays information about an asset's price movement. Candlestick charts are one of the most widely used components of technical analysis, allowing traders to interpret price information quickly through analyzing just a few price bars. A hammer can be used to show when there were selling pressures during the day, but a strong buying pressure later drove the price back up. The colour of the body can vary from green to red, but a green hammer indicates a stronger bull market than a red hammer.

TECHNICAL ANALYSIS INDICATORS

Using trading indicators is part of day trading technical strategy. When combined with the right risk management tools, it could help you gain more understanding of the price trends. Trading indicators are mathematical calculations usually plotted as lines on a price chart and can help traders extrapolate signals and trends within the financial market.

•Leading indicators: Provides users with future price fluctuations.

•Lagging indicators: Studies past trends and indicates exciting momentum.

The following are some identifiable trading indicators;

Simple Moving Average (SMA) Indicator: Used to extrapolate the direction of a current price trend, without any particular interruptions from a shorter-term price spike. The SMA indicator simply takes the price points of a financial accessory over a specific period and then divides it by the number of data points to present a single line trend. The data used actually depends on the length of the MA. For example, a 100-day MA requires 100 days of data. By using the MA indicator, you can determine possible future patterns.

Exponential Moving Average Indicator (EMA): EMA is another type of moving average indicator. But unlike the SMA, it factors a huge attention on recent data points, making data to be more responsive to new information. When rightly combined with other indicators, EMAs can help day traders analyse significant market moves and determine their legitimacy level. We have the 12- and 26-day EMAs for short-term averages, whereas the 50- and 200-day EMAs for long-term trend indicators.

Stochastic Oscillator: This is an indicator that compares a particular closing price of an asset to a range of its prices over time. It employs a scale of 0 to 100. A reading below 20 indicates an oversold market, while a reading above 80 shows an overbought market.

Moving Average Convergence Divergence Indicator: Helps traders identify potential buy and sell opportunities within support and resistance levels. 'Convergence' stands for when two moving averages are coming together, while 'divergence' stands for when they're moving away from each other. If moving averages are converging, it indicates momentum is decreasing, whereas if the moving averages are diverging, it shows that the momentum is increasing.

Bollinger Bands: Bollinger bands are useful when you want to know when an asset is trading outside of its normal levels, and are used most times as a means for predicting long-term price movements.

Relative Strength Index (RSI): RSI enables day traders to identify exciting momentum, market conditions and warning signals for dangerous price fluctuations. RSI is usually rated between 0 and 100. When an asset is around the 70 level, it is often considered overbought, while an asset at or very close to 30 is often regarded as oversold.

Fibonacci Retracement: Use to confirm whether there will be a move in price. It is an indicator that can show the extent to which a market will move against its current trend. A retracement occurs when the market undergoes a temporary dip. Also known as a pullback.

EFFECTIVE STEPS TO STARTING OUT A DAY TRADING BUSINESS

To become a successful day trader, you need to have a well-enough capital base and have access to a moderately cheap and functional trading platform.

The right trading mentality must be in you; otherwise, it will be somehow difficult to navigate your way successfully into the day trading niche.

A perfect understanding of market trends, financial securities, and behavioral psychology - alongside personal discipline and determination - are prerequisite for success.

The following are some of the thoroughly researched steps to becoming a successful day trader;

Conduct a thorough review of your personality: Ask yourself; do you have the right mindset? Can you work for longer hours doing research on the internet? Are you financially inclined? Are you a risk taker? Are you committed and dedicated to your purpose? If your answer is no, I'd advise you consider other niche for now.

Have a large capital base: This is so that if you run at a loss, you can still continue in the business. If you don't have a solid capital plan, your plan of becoming a successful day trader might fail.

Have a broad knowledge base relating to the financial market.

Understand trading and securities requirements.

Have a feasible trading strategy and be adaptable.

Know how to manage your resources, money especially.

Know much about brokerage services and plan ahead.

Don't invest all your worth. Begin small and grow in the process.

STEPS TO BUILD A WINNING TRADING PLAN

There's the cliché expression which has usually found its way into the lips of all and sundry - if you fail to plan, you have already started planning to fail. It is safe to say nothing works without proper planning. If you can imagine the level of planning that went into building Eiffel tower into what it is today, only then you can know planning brings beauty.

It is equally important to say that - just like every other thing in life - day trading requires sincere planning and dedication to progress. If you already have a workable plan to start your day trading career, it is all good. If you don't have such yet, you are not late.

Though your plans should not be entirely set in stones. That is, it must be one that is flexible and can adapt to market trends and fluctuations. Follow these steps;

Know your skills set and be ready to leverage on them.

Be emotionally, psychologically and financially ready. Don't be discouraged.

Don't invest all your earnings. If you have 50,000USD, you can set 30% for business.

Research your markets. You don't plough into anything that you don't really understand. Otherwise, you risk being burned out.

Set your targets. Know what you're expecting at the end of the day, and the strategy to achieve them.

Know when to enter the market.

Know when to exit the market.

Keep all records.

Stay clear and dedicated to your wants.

Chapter 6: What Is Day Trading?

Day trading is done on different platforms and systems, and the operator must be familiar with the trade. This should not scare you. To find out how it does not work in all cases, you need to be a computer expert. Learn to study the basic movements and technological development over time.

They lost the business market are attached; Most traders lose daily transactions. In general, they most often, they lose some money. It is also essential to focus and rationale for a period of losses and does not let the fundamental fact that money also lost. Focus on the future activities of daily transactions by implementing some of the strategies outlined in the grand scheme.

Independence is to build your own set of tools, which is always and Willy. Reading books Negotiate book, watch every video, interact with a mentor after the other can be a total lack. If the books have another point of confusion in your area? What is your YouTube subscriber who decides to leave the video running a blog? Always grasp the basics after a thorough study and sale of a vacation day. He dares you the pros and parts. But when you feel lost, do not hesitate to get help. More importantly, the teacher and analyze the success of movements and are part of his grand plan.

Good things take time. In a strategic move, do not try, think twice, but it should not cause paranoia. Act, by many areas to reduce the number of victims could be done in the various activities of daily transactions.

Also, the patient learns the day trader. Day trading will not be accessible at first, but over time, which will be equipped with a lot of skills and experience, it is expected that all is well. Hey, be patient.

Getting stuck in the past, which made many prisoners. Provident allowed to see the possible moves and gives a final air for future business activities will consider the requirements of a day trader. Continues to encourage visionary ahead, which is implies clear mental thinking about their next possible moves after careful consideration. Accelerates transactions being and simplifies future movements of daily operations and the chances are that you will succeed.

Day trading does not need to be a tycoon, but they must have a specific amount of money that has been specially selected to start the trading day. I remember the first days are always a win or a loss situation as you continue to learn and grow. This particular set of money can be lost as well. Be careful when handling your finances in day trading. Not every story is a good story.

High interest in something is the objective to hold successfully. Much enthusiastic tarpaulin, securities, products, markets, the company gives the desire to learn and master what day trading is all about. There are signs in the future entrepreneur.

The experience and knowledge.

Experience comes with a lot of the fall and learning. Exposure to various sources of learning and cost control every movement during the trading day, to squeeze the best. Getting real experience and knowledge of multiple platforms of negotiation and the strategies needed to succeed in trading is worth it.

The difference between short and long trade

On the stock markets, the long and short term usually means when trading begins for the first sale or purchase. The long workday starts after shopping in a store at a fixed price to sell at a higher price in the future, try to make a profit. In comparison, short transactions begin to sell before buying with the intention of his redemption at a lower market price and perhaps Acquire benefits.

Short selling is simple:

Ready for action.

Sell the shares.

Redemption of shares?

Gain or loss?

The risks are also involved in the sale; stock prices can be as high, and usually, there is no limit to how a price can go.

Long trade, the profit potential is unlimited, and asset prices can rise indefinitely.

Can you day trade for a living?

It should be removed as it may seem, day trading is a lucrative engagement. However, this does not mean that it is like any real work. So you have to be your boss. We will make your way at the time and their life strategies. He is incredible. Not so much happiness in this life, but also disadvantages appear. Then venture into the various advantages and disadvantages that come with day trading.

Advantages:

· Your boss

Learn to work the way you want; it has always been the best thing ever. His plan, their movements, their strategies. He is so good. Imagine, wanting to go on vacation without passing first through the human resources department for a great explanation of reasons can be quite significant. On the other hand, to come work for you and gives you all the power to do things alive. It has enough mind to learn and get the best of you. Do yourself a huge favor and be your boss.

· Comfort.

A quiet working environment improves the quality of the final product, but rather the consequences proved to be so useful. The peaceful atmosphere creates a workspace so focused, day traders to strictly control the actual activities of daily transactions and more each day. This will ultimately achieve its critical projects identified by the large portion of the profits to realize.

· Risk management.

Cases trading days of the day of exposure, without doubt, the best risk-taker. Day trading consists of many hazards, which act as day today. The merchant came to dominate the success and lay the old mistakes, to succeed as an entrepreneur.

· Technologically privileged.

Day Trading Internet exposes attempts to access a variety of sources. Internet technology is full of technology. You are exposed to new places and different technological techniques. It is built because the technology is present and the future.

Cons:

· Solitary lifestyle.

Day trading is quiet, which means the sound of physical activity should not be part of it. This creates a kind of lonely environment, especially as the business manager, for me to try to master the correct movements possible. You can take full advantage of the trading day; the best company is usually just your business.

· Incompatible salary.

Its intelligent commercial work will result in the form of compensation received by each trading day. If you decide to take a day off, the lack of promised benefits. At some point, you may experience day $ 3000 after the loss of $ 2000, and there are no uniform salary figures promised, his skillful movements are those that have a Lamborghini.

Decide what and when to buy.

When and how exactly to buy day trading is so fundamental. Let the point of some of the factors to consider.

Understanding the level of risk is involved and what level of risk is appropriate for you.

There are many activities for trade with idiosyncratic volatility, the price and volume. There are different types of risk experienced all levels of daily transactions.

As a beginner, choose the level of risk management of interest rate corresponding to the risk. Day of Action to the trading day, exposed to a variety of risks, which are often found in each trading day is a learning day. Over time, a beginner is exposed to all sorts of potential hazards that can be educational, and it becomes professional risk management.

Analyze and achieve the kind of purchase price.

Fully describing his personality, and so judge your car should encourage the kind of market you want to participate during the day. For example, if you have a quick mind, but I cannot focus regardless of the number of shares required in a given situation, you must go to short-term trading.

Development and analysis of concrete actions.

Keep it Simple. In particular, activities in time. Understanding how it is run, explore all the parties, and see how it works in different time intervals. Every action has its personality traits and the sense that you need to understand their behavior to predict the right moves.

Meet business graphics to understand the evolution of resources and overall market performance.

Graphics act as a graphical representation of the actual activities taking place in the market of daily transactions. Control of aid and to express every moment that takes place during the day. Beginners should learn and teach each movement is represented on maps of the future success of changes in the trading day.

Be disciplined and strictly follow the plan.

Monitor all initial strategic plan is successful in day trading. He is disciplined enough to follow what has been discussed and was taken by step; the contractor provides zero-day opportunity to get great loss pieces.

Period.

Traders spend about 30 seconds to select the time, not because of its technical and commercial business activities, but its personality. For example, operators who intend to do during the operation until the end of the day to choose shorter intervals, while entrepreneurs intend to do two to three services a day, especially negotiation Earn longer delays. Terms are not standing on the trading day of the activity of shopping that day says it all.

Deciding when to sell

Mental fatigue.

Business Incite long chains of brain fatigue poor stop losses match. Business forever States within two or three hours to play, and opportunities to excel in the industry are higher or lower.

Operating in the hole.

Novato is recommended not to participate in the first 15 minutes from the new trading day. It is considered the most experienced traders in this period a lot of money it stupid. The dumb money is nothing more than the actual amount of capital that the majority of traders buying and selling used as a market price based on previous episodes of redemptions at the beginning of the trading day. Professional players this morning is preferred.

Chapter 7: What Does Day Trading

Mean

The meaning of "day trading" is the purchasing and selling of a security in a solitary trading day. In case you're day trading on the web, you will finish off your situation before the markets close for the day to verify your benefits. You may likewise enter and leave different exchanges during a solitary trading session.

Representatives once in a while have various definitions for 'dynamic' or day traders. Their conclusion is regularly founded on the number of exchanges a customer opens or closes inside a month or year. A few brands even allude to 'hyper-dynamic traders' – a stage past the 'dynamic trader.'

Day trading is regularly done by utilizing trading strategies to benefit from little value developments in high-liquidity stocks or monetary standards. The reason for DayTrading.com is to give you a diagram of day trading nuts and bolts and the stuff for you to make it as a day trader. From scalping a couple of pips benefit in minutes on a forex exchange, to trading news occasions on stocks or lists – we clarify how.

What Can Be Traded?

The most worthwhile and famous day trading markets today are:

Forex – The remote trade cash market is the worlds generally famous and fluid. There are numerous momentary open doors in a slanting money pair and an unmatched degree of liquidity to guarantee to open and shutting exchanges is fast and smooth. Increasingly fit into the technical investigation, there are different approaches to exchange remote trade. What's more, forex has no focal market.

This implies traders can make exchanges six days every week, 24 hours per day. They present an extraordinary beginning stage for section level or hopeful traders with all-day employments. Traders in Australia may be explicitly keen on trading the AUD USD pair.

Stocks – Physical stocks in singular organizations, ordinary and Leveraged ETFs (a "Trade Traded Fund" holds different stocks or items and is exchanged like a solitary stock), prospects, and investment opportunities. Trading stocks intraday offers unexpected open doors in comparison to a conventional 'purchase and hold' strategy. Guessing on stock costs through CFDs or spread wagering, for instance, mean traders can benefit from falling costs as well. Edge or influences likewise lessen the capital required to open a position. So you can take a situation on the most recent news discharge, item declaration, or budgetary report – just as technical indicators.

Cryptocurrencies – The two most famous at present are Bitcoin and Ethereum. The money related vehicle existing apart from everything else. Fantastic development has seen cryptos draw in numerous new investors. Representatives are additionally guaranteeing retail access to these markets is less entangled. Obstructions to section are currently nearly nil, so whether you are a bull or a bear, this is the ideal opportunity.

Binary Options – The least complicated and most unsurprising technique, as the planning and profit for a productive exchange are known ahead of time. Administrative changes are pending, and with the division developing, large, settled brands currently offer these items. The primary inquiry for you is – will the benefit ascend in esteem, or not? With the drawback constrained to the size of the exchange and the potential payout known in cutting edge, understanding pairs aren't troublesome. They offer an alternative technique for trading and can influence at whatever day trader's day by day portfolio.

Futures – The future cost of awareness or security.

Commodities – Oil and gaseous petrol, nourishment kinds of stuff, metals, and minerals. In case you're S&P 500 day trading, you'll be purchasing and selling the portions of organizations, for example, Starbucks and Adobe.

File reserves as often as possible happen in monetary exhortation nowadays, yet are moderate budgetary vehicles that make them inadmissible for day by day exchanges. They have notwithstanding, been demonstrated to be extraordinary for long haul investing plans.

Beginning

Late reports show a flood in the quantity of day trading beginners. Be that as it may, not at all like the transient trading of the past, today's traders are more astute and better educated, to a limited extent because of trader institutes, courses, and assets, including trading applications. Daytrading.com exists to help amateur traders get taught and stay away from botches while figuring out how today's exchange.

Day trading 101 – find workable pace trading stocks or forex live utilizing a demo account first, they will give you essential trading tips. These free trading test systems will offer you the chance to learn before you put genuine money at risk. They likewise offer hands-on preparation on how to pick stocks.

It additionally implies swapping out your TV and different interests for instructive books and online assets. Find out about strategy and get a top to bottom comprehension of the perplexing trading world.

Loads of individuals regularly get puzzled by monetary terms, for example, money, for trade, trading, etc. It's a vast confusing money related globe just as among the fresh out of the box new trading thoughts is day trading.

Day trading, in its most essential term, shows procuring and marketing wellbeing and protections, supply just as different other financial speculations inside alone trading day it covers a broad scope of monetary things, for example, supplies, money, remote trade, value file, items just as prospects.

The monetary things that are brought are simply acknowledged a trading day just as must be cost fruition of a trading day.

Because of the short timeframe term in which to buy just as offer supplies, day trading is considered high-chance. On the off chance that you are keen on day trading, be set up to have enough assets.

Day trading is dangerous, and it has enormous motivations if you perceive precisely how to play right now. Various day investors never at any point grant themselves to acquire mental with any sort of one stockpile. When to decrease their misfortunes when the prerequisite happens just as ready to assess the present market design, particularly in the concise term, they have to perceive.

One advantage of day trading is that the intraday edge is 50 to 1. That suggests you are empowered to exchange roughly multiple times your first financing.

Imagine a scenario in which you don't have the necessary financing to spend in day trading. Luckily, you may endeavor day trading money.

One noteworthy drawback of day trading is the protections market is simply open for concerning 8 hours day by day. For money trading, the outside trade market is open all day, every day. That shows you can exchange nearly whenever of the day.

An extra advantage of day trading money is that a ton of day investors get an intraday edge of 4. That shows with precisely the same assets; you can exchange up to multiple times your assets.

Day trading monetary standards are furthermore a lot simpler to foresee just as watch out for differentiated to provisions as there are considerably less of them. Furthermore, the perspectives influencing overall remote trade market are negligible.

In day trading, you can shed huge alongside win huge done in a single day, so I would surely not propose any individual go through day trading up until you have a satisfactory experience and expertise in the stockpile or outside trade markets. Insightful just as quick decision creation is required notwithstanding the typical stock research study assessment, market assessment, etc.

Because of the limited timeframe span in which to buy and offer supplies, day trading is pondered hazardous. On the off chance that you are keen on day trading, be set up to have enough subsidizing. Consider the possibility that you don't have the required subsidizing to spend in day trading. One huge drawback of day trading is the inventory market is simply open for concerning 8 hours every day. An extra advantage of day trading money is that numerous day investors get an intraday edge of 4.

Some time ago, the main individuals who had the option to exchange effectively in the securities exchange were those working for huge money related organizations, businesses, and trading houses. With the ascent of the web and internet trading houses, agents have made it simpler for the average individual investor to get in on the game.

Day trading can end up being an exceptionally worthwhile profession, as long as you do it appropriately. However, it can likewise be a touch of trying for fledglings—particularly for the individuals who aren't completely arranged with a very much arranged strategy. Indeed, even the most prepared day traders can hit harsh fixes and experience misfortunes. All in all, what precisely is day trading, and how can it work?

THE FEATURES

Day traders are dynamic traders who execute intraday strategies to benefit off value changes for a given resource.

Day trading utilizes a wide assortment of systems and strategies to gain by apparent market wasteful aspects.

Day trading is regularly described by technical investigation and requires a high level of self-control and objectivity.

The Basics of Day Trading

Day trading is characterized as the buy and offer of security inside a solitary trading day. It can happen in any marketplace; however, it is generally basic in the outside trade (forex) and financial exchanges. Day traders are commonly accomplished and very much subsidized. They utilize high measures of use and transient trading strategies to gain by little value developments in exceptionally fluid stocks or monetary standards.

Day traders are receptive to occasions that cause momentary market moves. Trading the news is a well-known strategy. Planned declarations, for example, financial insights, corporate profit, or loan fees, are liable to market desires and market brain research. Markets respond when those desires are not met or are surpassed, as a rule with unexpected, noteworthy moves, which can profit day traders.

Day traders utilize various intraday strategies. These strategies include:

Scalping, which endeavors to make various little benefits on little costs changes for the day

Range trading, which fundamentally utilizes backing and obstruction levels to decide their purchase and sell choices

News-based trading, which regularly holds onto trading openings from the increased volatility around news occasions

High-recurrence trading (HFT) strategies that utilization refined calculations to

misuse   little   or   momentary   market
wasteful aspects

Chapter 8: Day Trading Strategy 6 –

Opening Range Breakout

Now it is time to look at another popular trading strategy that you can work with, known as the opening range breakout. This strategy is a good one for beginners because it can signal a point for entry, but you will find it doesn't tell you where you should target your profit. You can pick out the profit you want to reach based on other strategies that are in this guidebook. The opening range breakout is just to be used as an entry signal, but if you use the rules for trading, then you need to come up with your own exit point as well.

To work with the opening range breakout, you should pay attention to what is going on in the market. When you look at the charts during this time, you will notice that the Stocks in Play go through a violent price action. Buyers and sellers are flooding the market right when it opens and the first five minutes can be a crazy time. New investors and traders will also choose to get into the market right when it opens for the day.

Some investors will look at this time and notice that their chosen position went down through the night. They may panic if they don't realize what is going on and sell off their stocks. There are plenty of new investors who come in and see that the stock is at a low price. They will jump onto that stock before the price of that stock goes back up. Both of these movements are important because they are going to determine the stock's price and where it will go during that day.

As a day investor who will not hold onto their position for more than a day, you will want to wait out the beginning of the markets open. Wait at least five minutes before you choose which stock to invest in. When all those sellers or buyers enter the market, it is hard to determine who is going to become the winner in the market. You don't want to guess wrong during this crazy time and it is best to wait at least a few minutes to make sure you can see the solid trends in the market before investing.

Once this opening period is over, the trader can work on the plan they want to use for trading. For this strategy, you want to do a plan that is based on either half an hour to an hour breakout. There are some that like to work with a smaller time frame such as fifteen minutes. The longer the time frame that you choose to work on with this strategy, the less volatility so often this is easier for a beginner to use.

Like with many of the other setups that we have talked about in this guidebook, the opening range breakout strategy is going to work the best with either mid-cap or large stocks or ones that won't go through huge and unpredictable price swings while you hold onto them. You also want to make sure that you don't go into this type of strategy with some low float stocks.

Pick out a stock that has the ability to trade inside a range smaller than the ATR, or the Average True Range.

Working with the opening range breakout strategy, there are a few steps that you will need to follow. These steps include:

After you have had some time to create your watchlist in the morning, you should wait until the stock market has time to settle down, so wait about five minutes. During this time, watch the price action and the opening range. You can also check out how many shares are traded during that time and then figure out from that information if the stock is going down or up. This time is when a ton of orders go through the market and you want to look at these numbers to see how liquid a stock actually is.

During this time, you can also look through to see what the ATR of that stock is. You want the opening range to be smaller compared to the ATR so make sure the ATR number is nearby.

Once those first five minutes of the market opening are finished, you may see that the stock will stay in that opening range a bit longer depending on what traders and investors want to do. However, if you see at this time that the stock is breaking out of this range, it is time to enter the trade. Enter the trade going the same direction of the breakout. If you can, go long if you see the breakout is going up, but go short if the breakout is going down.

Pick out a good target for your profit as well. You can find this by looking at the daily levels from the previous day and identify where the stock is before the market opens. You can also look at the previous days' close, along with the moving averages, to come up with a good target.

If you can't find the right technical level for your chosen target or for the exit, you can choose to go long and then look for signs of weakness. On the other hand, if you want to take a short position, and then the stock goes high, this shows you the stock is strong and you want to cover the position as much as you can.

This method is going to work when you are doing the opening range and can work with any time frame that you want such as fifteen minutes or half an hour, but the steps above are for a five-minute trade. You will have to watch the market and find out what is the best opening range breakout depending on the market you are working with.

The opening range breakout is one that works well and can help ensure that you won't be fooled by any changes that occur right when the market opens that morning. But you do get the option to use it to look at how the market is doing for the day. Just make sure that when you do the opening range breakout, you don't trade during the first five to ten minutes or you may be caught in the wrong side of things.

The beginning of the market can be really volatile and it just isn't a good idea to jump on during this time. But after the opening of the market is done, you will be able to move into the market and utilize the breakouts that occur after it is done.

Chapter 9: Choosing Which Stocks

To Trade

Now that you have established your trading plan, you can start your research on which securities you will trade with it. There are several different securities that can be traded with a day trading method, including stocks, currencies, options, ETFs and mutual funds. All of these trade differently and having an understanding of how each behaves in the marketplace is critical before beginning trading. Here, we will focus mainly on stocks, as they are a very common security for day trading.

There are literally thousands of stocks available for trade on any given day, and each moves within the market uniquely. How do you decide which stock or stocks to trade? Do you simply go after the most popular and widely traded like Google and

Apple? Or do you just go after IPOs and hope for a quick flip? Finding the best stocks to trade based on your methodology is going to require a bit of research. The following steps will help you through it:

Create your watch list

Since there are so many stocks to trade, you can't possibly watch them all daily. Before you really get going, create a list of stocks whose movements you can monitor. It is best to choose one or two sectors then choose a few stocks from each to put on your watch list. Some of the most popular sectors are:

Banking

Precious Metals

Semiconductor

Automotive

Pharmaceuticals

Retail

Internet

Choose one or two sectors that you would like to follow then track the movement of the top issues. Limit the number of stocks that you follow to about 10 per sector, maxing out at 20 stocks being monitored at a time. This will allow you to truly track and understand their movement trends.

Get an early start on Trading Day

Day trading is not going to be conducive to flopping into your desk chair 10 minutes before the market opens. The market moves fast and you need to have your day plan established before it opens. Getting started early, at least an hour or two before market open, gives you an opportunity to do your research and configure your monitors with the stocks you will trade that day.

Once you have your cup of coffee and have settled into your desk, begin to analyze the pre-market. If you've been involved in the market for a while, you know not to place any gambles based solely on pre-market movement, as the swings can be drastic. However, doing a scan will give you a place to start when choosing which stocks to work with that day. Here is a guideline for what to look for:

Stocks priced over $5. If you have placed tight stops on your plan (and you should have), stocks that are priced below this mark will not give you much wiggle room during the trade.

Look for stocks with somewhat heavy volume. A stock may show that it is up 25%, but if it's only on 200 shares, you should move right along.

Once you have found a stock in the correct price range that is positive on a reasonable volume, review the volume average over the last 30 days. This will give you an idea of how the stock usually trades and whether it is a good candidate for day trading.

At this point, you will also want to review the broad market for the major indices.

Trade High Volume Stocks

It is advisable to trade on stocks that have a high enough volume that you can quickly enter and exit trades. Your brokerage account will likely provide a "most active" list which will give you the top 10 or 20 highest volume stocks; that is a great place to start. Finding a screener that will go beyond this ranking, though, will be advantageous as it will allow you a broader list and possibly stocks that are not being tracked by every investor. It is also a good idea to look at stocks that are rising on high volume relative to themselves. If a stock usually trades 3 million shares per day, but today has 5 million shares traded by market open, this is certainly something worth exploring.

Monitor the Earnings Calendar

Before delving any further into this, be advised that it is very ill-advised to place trades before earnings are posted. Pre-positioning yourself for earnings announcements is just another form of gambling. Reporting of earnings, however, is one event that increases volatility and knowing who will be reporting that week gives you an idea of who the likely movers will be.

Check out Social Media

Social Media has crept into so many aspects of all our lives, why not investment strategy as well? There are now social media streams that will give you another method for scanning the market. StockTwits and StockCharts are two forums that stream real-time information on which stocks are being discussed and which charts are being monitored. This could give you an idea of market movement that other traders are seeing first. Be careful when making decisions using these platforms, however, since you don't always know the validity of the sources. They would be best regarded as a jumping off point for doing your own research.

A final word on choosing stocks: If the above seems like a lot of work (because it is) and you would rather master something a little more simple, consider trading the same one or two stocks every day and learn to understand their movements. You could simply choose one of the most popular stocks with a lot of volume (like Google or Apple). This will be a little less stressful than reacting daily to market action and allows you to learn the trading pattern and identify the technical indicators for that particular security.

Overall, for a day trader the two most important qualities in a stock are liquidity and volatility. Tight spreads with low slippage (the difference between the expected price of a stock and the actual price), combined with the right amount of volatility create the perfect environment for lucrative trading.

Chapter 10: Fundamental Analysis

Fundamental Analysis

In order to successfully trade in the forex market, one of the most important things you are going to need to learn is to determine a reliable way to tell a potentially profitable trade from one that is likely to fizzle out or, even worse, cost you money. This is where proper analysis comes into play either through technical analysis (outlined below) or via fundamental analysis. Fundamental analysis is used more frequently by new traders, while technical analysis has experienced something of a renaissance in popularity over the past decade or so. While both are useful when it comes to finding the information you are looking for, they go about determining just what that information is in different ways. Fundamental analysis is primarily concerned with looking at the big picture, which often means that it will take longer to perform than its counterpart.

Additionally, its information comes from external sources which means you may need to wait for additional information to become available though it will typically end up being easier to digest than the information required to utilize technical analysis effectively. Broadly, fundamental analysis makes it easier for you to glimpse the likely future of the forex market based on a wide variety of different variables including publicized changes to the monetary policy of the countries you are interested in. The end goal is to track down enough information to allow you to find an undervalued currency pair that the market has not adjusted to.

Determine the baseline: When it comes to considering the fundamental aspects of a currency pair, you will first want to consider the baseline that these currencies typically return to time after time when compared to the other currency pairs that are commonly traded. This will make it easier to determine when the right time to make a move is likely to be as you will then be more easily able to pinpoint changes that occur to the pair that make them warrant additional consideration.

In order to determine this baseline, the first thing you will need to consider is any changes to the related macroeconomic policy that affects each based on historical data. In these instances, past behavior is one of the most reliable indicators when it comes to determining likely future events. Once you are aware of the relevant historical context you will then need to consider the current phase that the currency is in and how likely it is to remain in the phase in question as opposed to moving on to the next.

Each currency regularly goes through 6 distinct phases, the first of which is the boom phase which can be identified via low volatility and large amounts of liquidity. At the opposite end of the spectrum is the bust phase which can be identified by the opposite, mainly low amounts of liquidity and high amounts of volatility. The other phases are post-bust and pre-bust and post-boom and pre-boom which means that one of the major phases is either on its way in or on its way out. Determining the proper phase is crucial when it comes to ensuring that you are on the right track when it comes to finding a trading pair that is likely to be profitable in the long-term.

In order to determine the current phase, the easiest way to go about doing so is by looking at the current number of defaults along with bank loans as well as the accumulated reserve levels of the related currencies. If the numbers are low then a boom phase is likely on its way or possibly in full swing already. If the current numbers have already overstayed their welcome then you can be confident that a post-boom phase is likely to start at any time. Alternatively, if the numbers in question are higher than the baseline you have already established then you know that the currency is likely either due for a bust phase or is already underway.

Money can be made regardless of the current phase as long as you can capitalize on it before the market catches up as it is typically fairly slow moving.

Worldwide considerations: After you have an understanding of the baseline the currency pairs you are working with tend to remain at, the next thing you will want to do is to determine is what the related global economic conditions are likely to be and how they are going to affect your trading pair. In order for this to be effective, you are going to want to look beyond the obvious signals and dig deep to find the indicators that are surely going to make waves after they become public knowledge. One of the best ways to go about doing so is to looking into emerging technologies in the related countries as they can easily turn entire economies on their heads in a relatively short period of time.

Technological indicators are a great way to use a boom phase to its full advantage as by getting in on the ground floor you can ride the wave for as long as it takes for that technology to become a full-fledged part of the mainstream. After it reaches the saturation point then you are going to want to be on the lookout for the bust phase as it will likely be right around the corner. If you feel as though the countries related to the currencies in question will soon be in a post-bust or post-boom phase then you will want to think twice about moving into speculative markets as the drop off is sure to be coming and it can be difficult to determine exactly when it will rear its ugly head.

If you feel confident that a phase shift is on the horizon but you don't know when it will be exactly then you are going to want to stick with smaller leverage points than you would during the other phases to ensure that they will pay out before the change occurs. On the other hand, if a phase is just starting then you will want to go ahead and make riskier trades as the time concerns aren't going to come into play which means extra caution is less warranted.

Global implications: While regional concerns are a good place to start, it is also important to take a macro view of the market as a whole, as global currency policies are almost always likely to play a part in the proceedings. While it might be difficult to determine where you should start, at first, all you really need to do is to apply the same level of analysis that you have performed on the micro level, just on a larger scale. The best place to start is generally going to be with the interest rates of the major players on the world stage include the Federal Reserve, the European Central Bank, the Bank of England and the Bank of Japan.

You will also need to be aware of any policy biases or legal mandates that are currently making the rounds in order to ensure that you don't end up getting blindsided from these sources when it comes time for you to make your move. While this will certainly be time consuming work, understanding the market from all sides will make it easier to determine new emerging markets when specific areas are fat with supply growth and what the expectations regarding interest rate changes or market volatility are soon going to be.

Understand the past: After you have a clear idea of what the current state of the worldwide economy is looking like, along with the specifics regarding the currency pairs you are interested in trading, then the next thing you will need to do is look to the past so that you can be prepared for history to repeat itself. This level of understanding will make it easier for you to understand the current strength of your respective currencies while also allowing you to more accurately determine the length of time you can expect the current phase to continue.

In order to capitalize on this knowledge in the most effective way possible, you are going to want to attempt to jump onto trades when one of the currencies is entering a post-bust phase while the other is in the midst of a post-boom phase. When this occurs, credit channels will not yet be exhausted and you will be able to take advantage of the greatest amount of risk possible when compared to any other market state.

Be aware of volatility: Being aware of the current level of volatility is crucial when it comes to ensuring that the investments you are making are likely to actually pay out in your favor. This is relatively easy to do, all you need to do is to pay attention to the stock markets most closely related to the currencies you favor.

This is because the forex market tends to be more stable, the more stable the stock market is because the lower the perceived overall risk is, the lower the amount of perceived risk that can make its way to the forex market.

Remember, the closer to the peak of the boom phase you currently find yourself, the lower interest rates, default rates, and volatility will be which means it is the best time to increase your level of risk. Alternately, the closer you find yourself to the bust phase, the higher the overall level of volatility, default and interest rates are going to be.

Decide on the best currency pairs: With a good idea of where the market currently is and how long it is likely to stay there, all that you have left to do is determine the most effective currency pairs to actually sell. To do this you must first consider any gap between the 2 currencies when it comes to interest rates. You need to have a clear understanding of where each of the pair are currently and how likely they are going to remain close together and with a proper distribution between them.

To find this information you are going to want to start by looking at the difference in the output gap as well as related unemployment statistics. When capacity constraints increase, while at the same time unemployment decreases, this shortage will lead to an inflated economy, which in turn, will cause interest rates will rise until the economy begins to cool. Charting this information will allow you to accurately determine the likely interest rate movement from the pair in question.

Additionally, you will want to consider the payment balance of the nations related to the currencies in question. The healthier the debt to capital ratio, the stronger the related currency is likely to remain in times of crisis. To determine this amount, you are going to want to consider the capital as well as the current account and the general situation of each. This will help you to determine if the position the nation in question is holding is due to asset sales or bank deposits or other, long term potential developments including things like an accumulation of reserves or foreign investment.

Economic indicators to watch

When it comes to major economic indicators, the list is a fairly short one. Unfortunately, if you hope to stay competitive in the forex market then you are going to need to keep up with far more than just the basics. This is easier said than done, however, as there are a huge variety of economic surveys and other relevant indicators that can be used to predict numerous types of trends before they happen. While the entire list is too massive to include in its entirety, the options listed below will get you started on the right track.

This is because, rather than simply present the reader with raw data, it instead uses a tone that is much more conversational as it describes the various regional goings on of the various members of the United States Federal banking districts. This allows traders to determine how the Fed comes to various conclusions in various circumstances which, in turn, can be useful later on when it comes to making bets on how the currency will move in the future.

This economic indicator is published prior to each Federal Open Market Committee Meeting, which works out to be 8 times per year.

While the beige book does not typically crate that much of a commotion as it doesn't present anything strictly new, instead, it helps to point knowledgeable traders in the likely direction that things are going to be moving in the future. For example, if the overall tone of a beige book indicates a growing worry about inflation, then you might be able to start making preliminary plans related to a decrease in the current USD interest rate.

Consumer price index: A consumer price index is a sort of benchmark for a specific country's economy and its current level of inflation. It utilizes a basket approach as it attempts to compare a steady base of products that don't change much from year to year. These products include many common items including toiletries and other common groceries in addition to everyday services like the price of a haircut or an oil change.

These numbers tend to be broken down into a handful of figures, the first of which is broken down into two categories known as the Urban Wage Earners and the Clerical Workers. The second category is known as Urban Consumers. The consumer price index for a given set of urban consumers is often tracked quite closely as it varies dramatically throughout the year. In the US, the current percentage is shown in comparison to the year 1982 so changes can only be determined based on previous index levels. Numbers are then shown via a run rate of grown to show traders what they can expect from inflation as well.

Meanwhile, the chain-weighted consumer price index often sees a major push when it comes to relevancy. This index provides a numerical visualization of customer purchasing patterns when compared to other indexes. As an example, only the chain weighted index notes things like when the public shifts from one brand to another based on things like price increases.

In addition to major economic indicators like these, the consumer price index is often viewed by many trades as the final say when it comes to the up to date financial situation of a given country. It is released once per month and when it is you can count on serious movement for any related currency pairs.

Durable Goods Report: This report is released monthly and provides valuable updates when it comes to the amount of manufacturing that is being done in a given country when it comes to durable goods. A durable good is any type of capital good that has an average lifespan of more than three years. Nearly 100 different industries fall under this report's purview including things like cars, semiconductors and even wind turbines. The figures for a given country will be provided in the currency of that company along with a percentage of change for the month over month numbers. Three months of revisions are also included in every report. Data from this report is one of the 10 core components of the US Conference Board Leading Index which is used to divine future movement in the global market.

When it comes to reading these reports it is vital that you always remember that the numbers that are publicly reported often do not include transportation goods or items created by the defense sector as they tend to be volatile enough to skew things dramatically one way or the other. Thus, if you want the full story on a given country you will need to do your due diligence and sniff these numbers out for yourself.

Generally speaking, the durable goods report is an excellent way for savvy traders to get a viable overview of business demand in specific countries. This is the case because these types of capital goods tend to require a larger overall investment which, in turn, shows that business owners and consumers are both acting with greater confidence than they would be if the economy was not moving in a positive direction.

Based on the results you find you may also find it especially useful to consider topics like the variation that occurs when it comes to inventory and shipment ratios over a prolonged period of time in addition to the growth rate of shipments and related inventories. Taken together, these should provide a much clearer picture of whether or not supply is exceeding demand or vice versa. As these types of goods often take far longer to be created than more transient goods, the durable goods report can also be an excellent way to get an early read on the expected earnings increases for the future month as an influx of orders in one month is a good sign that additional growth will be forthcoming.

Employment cost index: The employment cost index is a useful economic indicator that is released four times per year. It focuses on the amount that businesses in a given country pay for each employee, on average, as well as how much that has changed over the proceeding quarter. This report looks at things like employee benefits, hourly wages, bonuses and any relevant employee premiums for every industry besides government and farm labor as these would skew the numbers at either end of the spectrum.

This data is then broken down on an industry by industry basis before being split even further based on whether or not the industry is unionized. This information tends to also be broken down industry by industry which makes it especially useful to traders who are looking for early indicators when it comes to determining potential signs of inflation. This is due to the fact that the cost for compensating employees is the greatest cost almost any industry faces and they tend to be presented in terms of the cost to the company in relation to the amount of profit that is generated when it comes to particular goods and services that are being generated.

Based on its overall outlook, the employee cost index can actually be enough to change the direction of a specific currency completely. This will occur if the actual report comes back in such a way that it is dramatically different from what all estimates expected. This is because these types of compensation costs are almost always passed off onto consumers which leads to further GDP projection reductions when it is left untreated in the long-term. This is also one of several indicators that is useful when it comes to determining a country's overall assumed level of productivity. If productivity grows at a slower rate than the rate at which compensation costs are increasing, then the valuation of the related currency is going to decrease and vice versa.

Focus on interest rates: After you have a clear idea of the market as a whole and major currencies specifically, you are going to want to focus on what many traders in the forex market focus on the most, the difference in interest rates between various currencies. This is a crucial step if you hope to form an accurate opinion on the strengths of various relevant central banks, which in turn factors into an accurate qualitative analysis of the situation as a whole.

To form a clearer picture in this regard you are going to want to consider the unemployment statistics of both countries as well as the gap in output that each has. If the economy is increasing, while at the same time, available labor is decreasing, then this will eventually lead to inflation and overall higher rates. This, in turn, will lead to higher rates from the central bank which will keep them there until the economy starts heading in the other direction. Keeping an eye on these trends will leave you with a clear idea of what your qualitative analysis has revealed.

Take stock of each country's external position: When it comes to getting the proper feel for a currency or currency pair it is important to keep in mind how healthy their balance of payments currently is. If one of the countries in question has a position that is generally considered to be maintained via asset sales and bank deposits, which can dry up or change direction relatively quickly, then that is less reassuring than a country with long term commitments such as reserve accumulation or foreign direct investment.

Chapter 11: Intermediate Trader

Tools

When it comes to improving the trading tools you are currently using, if you are just starting out then one of the most important things to consider is how much a specific tool or site membership is actually going to benefit you versus what it is going to cost. With that being said, all of the tools listed below are available for free.

Stock Chart Websites

Stock Charts (StockCharts.com): This site is one of the best around thanks to its easy scalability, cleanliness and simplicity. It is lauded for it large number of free tools and analyzing options. Historical charting and additional analysis options are also available if you are interested in upgrading to a paid subscription.

Trading View (TradingView.com): This site offers a variety of options when it comes to displaying individual charts. These charts are driven by the community and often come with annotations made by veteran traders with the goal of helping new traders learn. It also offers lots of flexibility and a cheaper premium subscription when compared with Stock Charts.

Google Finance (Finance.Google.com): This site, powered by Google, offers a clean and minimalized charting solution for traders who are just interested in the bare data. One of its best features is its ability to allow you to pinpoint when major events occurred by analyzing historical performance. It also offers extremely easy point by point comparison thanks to the ability to make charts overlap.

FINVIZ (FINVIZ.com): This site is unique among free options in that it includes a technical analysis overlay on charts by default. It also offers few adds and simple and clear charts and a wide variety of tools available without the need of a premium subscription.

Technical Analysis Tools

Stockalyze (Stockalyze.com): This is a software suite with a paid, as well as a detailed free version. It includes the ability to create end of day charts and track a variety of types of data with over 50 types of indicators to choose from including MFI, RSI, ADX, MACD, Bollinger Band and Moving Averages. It also offers numerous trading systems as well as the ability to make your own. Finally, you can also use it to create charts to point and figure.

Incredible Charts (IncredibleCharts.com): This free software allows you to chart candlestick charts, point and figure charts as well as equivolume charts. It also includes proprietary indicators such as Twiggs Money Flow, Twiggs Momentum Oscillator, Fibonacci sequencing, and other trend channel tools. It also offers a 30-day trial of its premium market data service which includes Dow Jones, CBOE, World indices, Forex, Precious Metals, ASX, TSX, LSE and TSX venture exchanges as well as the NYSE, NASDAQ, OTC and OTCBB markets.

Technical Analysis- Free Software (Freeware.intrastar.net): This isn't so much a single software download as it is a wide variety of free programs which can handle pretty much everything you would ever need to do in conjunction with trading regularly. Before you go out and pay for any software, do yourself a favor and scan this site for a free approximation instead.

Chapter 12: Wealth Creation

Strategies

An Introduction to Dollar Cost Averaging

The average dollar cost term is a strategy used by both merchants and investors to buy similar dollar investments over specific periods. This strategy allows operators to regularly buy investments of a particular cost to increase their investments. Under this strategy, assets are purchased regardless of price.

When you start investing, you will probably come across this term. The dollar average is a strategy that has existed for quite some time. There is general acceptance by experts that investors who implement this strategy regardless of different conditions, such as markets and at set intervals, tend to perform much better than people who invest emotionally. Emotional investors tend to be overconfident one minute and panic mode the next. Because of this, they tend to expose themselves to numerous risks, especially when they don't have a proper investment plant, but are simply guided by their emotions.

The best part regarding this strategy is that it eliminates the emotions of investing. You can spend regardless of how you feel. This is highly recommended because emotions tend to ruin the investment and cause considerable losses to investors.

Understand the average cost in dollars

Rather than an investor putting a lump sum of money into assets, this approach requires a different approach. An investor will generally place small but regular amounts in various investments and then increase these amounts periodically.

This allows you to spread the cost base and enable the investor to slowly invest their funds in smaller amounts over a couple of months or years. This ensures that the investment portfolio is protected and isolated from different situations, especially in a constantly changing market.

For example, when prices are rising rapidly in the stock market, the investor will end up paying much more than other occasions. However, the opposite is exact when markets are slow. The investor will be able to increase his investment at low prices and, therefore, isolate himself. This is the benefit of using this specific investment strategy.

How Dollar Cost Averaging Works

Dollar-cost, as defined above, is an investment tool used by fund managers, investors, and other participants in the stock market to generate wealth or savings over an extended period. This strategy provides a way to manage and possibly neutralize and possible volatility, at least in the short term in all markets. The application of this is evident in 401 (K) accounts.

401 (K) account holders can choose a pre-agreed amount of their payment to invest in the index or the mutual funds of their choice. This amount will be deducted from your refund as a fixed but regular amount remitted monthly to your 401 (K) account. Applying this investment strategy beyond 401 (K) accounts and other investment opportunities, such as an index or mutual funds, is possible. Investors can also use the same strategy to invest in dividend investment plans through regular contributions.

Therefore, instead of investing large sums of money in an investment, an investor will work slowly but surely in a placement through small but regular contributions spread over set periods. There are certain benefits associated with this investment approach.

One of the outstanding benefits of using this investment strategy is that the cost base spans several years and at variable prices. This helps to ensure that there is sufficient insulation against any future market price changes. Also, it implies that investors will experience a higher cost base during times of rapidly rising stock prices than during regular stock price movements.

How to set up an investment plan

There is a way for an investor to plan his life so that he can invest in using the dollar-cost averaging strategy. To achieve this, the investor must accomplish three main things. These are listed below.

1. Determine the amount of money you want to set aside each month or each pay period for investment purposes. As an investor, you need to make sure that this is an amount that you can reserve comfortably and without putting pressure on your lifestyle. This amount should also be cautious because if it is too small, it will not be of much use.

2. The next step is to establish an investment as a 401 (K) where the funds will go. Please note that these funds are very likely to be held for a long time, so it

is crucial to make sure that no reserved money will be needed to cover essential items such as rent or bill payment, etc. The funds are often invested for five to ten years. It is advisable to think about this period before choosing this investment strategy.

3. Remember that the payment intervals can be of any duration but not standard. These intervals can be monthly, weekly, or quarterly, depending on various factors, such as the frequency of payment. This money is invested in a security or fund that the client wants. Most of the time, an investor will set up an automated payment system that automatically deducts funds and then makes them available to the fund, etc. Sometimes, investors work with brokers, but it is possible to invest without using a broker's services.

For example, on how to set up an average dollar cost opportunity, Jayden is an employee of the XYZ firm and has signed a 401 (K) plan. Your employer pays you a net salary of $ 2,000 per fortnight. Jayden makes a conscious decision to set aside 10% of his biweekly investment payment. He elects to commit 50% of this 10% toward an employer-proposed retirement plan. He then decides to remit the rest to an S&P-based Index Fund. You'll spend $ 100 on your employer's plan and another $ 100 to the Index Fund.

Transcendence

The dollar-cost averaging strategy has been evident and accessible in 401 (K) accounts. The people and organizations that invest in these accounts do so regardless of market conditions. In the long term, this approach is beneficial in many ways, and, least of all, the low overall cost of investment.

There is only one significant drawback related to this strategy. If a bubble occurs in the stock market, or if you enter a position in the market where there is a substantial increase in value, the costs related to the investment will be much higher than would have been the case.

Building an Investment Portfolio

As an investor, diversification is the best approach. Diversification means investing your funds in different securities. This is highly recommended due to the inherent and underlying risks posed by the markets. It is a fact that the price or value of the shares changes almost all the time. Putting all your eggs in one basket is a risky affair in case things go wrong. Diversification means that whatever happens, it can still be profitable. Therefore, to invest wisely, you will need to develop or create a suitable investment portfolio. It's easy to imagine an investment portfolio where all of your investments take place. A wallet is, in other ways, similar to a safe that stores crucial personal or business documents. However, unlike a safe,

When you diversify your investments in a portfolio, you will have a large number of assets. These assets could be ETFs, mutual funds, bonds, stocks, and many others. However, it is better to approach the diversification of a portfolio with a well thought out plan and not at random.

Principles for building a portfolio

We can define portfolio management as an approach to balance rewards and risks. To meet your investment objectives, you.

We will need to invest in a wide variety of products, including SMA, REIT, closed-end funds, ETFs, and others. It is an excellent idea and highly recommended to have an investment plan and determine your ultimate goal, especially when there are so many options available.

Portfolio management often means different things to different investors. Think of a young man new to college and his first job. Such a person views portfolio management as a way to increase investments and provide a reasonably decent amount over time for future use. On the other hand, a not-so-young person who has been working or in business for a while will see things differently. Such a person will see portfolio management as an excellent opportunity to preserve their possibly accumulated wealth over the years. There are different ways to organize and plan portfolio management.

A portfolio manager must be able to handle the diverse needs that different investors have when building a diversified portfolio. That is why the individualized approach is a highly recommended option. Here are some basic principles for developing a portfolio.

First, it is advisable to consider the availability of numerous options. This means that there are many investment vehicles to choose from. Therefore, a client or investor must determine if they want to create wealth over time, save funds for future use, generate a regular income, etc. In this way, it will be possible to prepare an adequate investment plan. Such a plan should incorporate risk appetite, time frame, and the like.

Some basic strategies

One of the first steps in establishing a portfolio is to present an informed but realistic perspective on the best approach to investing funds wisely and productively. The best way is to start from the end goal and formulate a strategy that supports the achievement of this goal. It is advisable to consider all the associated risks, as well as the time factor for the wishes of an investor to be fulfilled.

When we talk about the time frame, we refer to when an initial investment is made and the time until the investor needs to access the same funds. Therefore, the initial steps involve developing a preliminary plan that includes a selection of different products and accounts.

Another essential factor to keep in mind is that the findings must be diversified across various asset classes and different sectors. Once funds are distributed to different industries and asset classes, there should be regular monitoring of each asset's performance. If necessary, adjustments should be made as appropriate.

Goal achievements

When investments are made in the right way, adequately diversified across different asset classes and sectors, achieving all of the stated objectives will be possible. Investors have short-term goals, medium-term goals, and long-term goals. Short-term goals may involve furnishing a home, saving for a vacation or buying a motor vehicle, etc. Long-term investment goals could be to keep to start a business, buy a home, and even save for retirement. It could also include saving for children's college. For these reasons, it is advisable to monitor portfolio performance for adjustments if deemed necessary regularly. In some cases, objectives change and regular portfolio monitoring.

Financial advisory services

One of the best ways to invest and harness the power of informed investments is to work with a portfolio manager or any other financial expert. Indeed, many investors invest independently without the help of professionals. However, working with a professional makes it easy to diversify funds across different sectors and asset classes to monitor investment performance over time.

Investors on their own will lack the kind of exposure, assistance, and wisdom that investment managers and financial advisers have. As an investor, you must have adequate information about all the tools and systems available to you. You should also know every emerging opportunity, as well as access to all available resources. This is advisable only for those who know what they are doing, including finance experts, accountants, bankers, etc.

On the other hand, while professional investment advice is crucial for ordinary investors, it is not free. There is a fee to be paid. Investors have to pay expenses, such as consultation fees, to receive professional investment advice. However, the benefit obtained through professional consultations is invaluable. The expert has not only knowledge and experience, but also an intimate understanding of finance and the various sectors. Also, financial advisers have a legal responsibility or fiduciary duty to clients, which means that they must work in the best interest of their clients.

There are financial planners, and then there are brokers. Brokers often buy securities on behalf of clients. They act more as intermediaries between clients and companies that trade with funds. On the other hand, we have investment advisers. They are professionals who provide advice and recommendations on the best investment vehicles.

Division of funds for the portfolio

When it comes to finally choose the funds and amounts to be allocated to each type of fund or asset, there are specific considerations that must be made. First, you should consider any investment objective, such as short and long term objectives. Others include the preferred rate of return, time available, etc. It is possible to find mutual funds designed for each situation. Therefore, investors should take the time to examine the various funds and sometimes even different instruments in multiple sectors before finally choosing their preferred one.

Inclusions in an investment portfolio

Once you start investing, there are certain assets that you will need to invest in. You may have to open and manage multiple accounts due to the need for diversification. Some of the reports you can open and invest in include an individual retirement account, a 401 (K) account, or another type of employer-sponsored account, a brokerage account, peer-to-peer loan accounts, etc. Even investing in cash in certificates of deposit and the money markets are welcome forms of diversification.

These accounts, whichever is selected, must have a variety of assets. These include futures, retirement funds, options, mutual funds, REIT, and many others. While diversification is crucial to a successful investment, investors should avoid expensive investments and any assets that carry uncertainty. It is better to choose investment options like low-cost index funds. Ideally, most funds should be invested in ETFs and mutual funds. The reason for this is that these reflect significant indices, such as the Dow Jones Industrial Average and the S&P 500. It is a cost-saving approach to diversify a portfolio.

Diversification also refers to investing in a variety of unrelated assets. Take bonds and stocks, for example. These have a negative correlation because when one asset class increases, the other will probably decrease in price and vice versa.

The golden rule in pricing

When it comes to pricing, the general rule is to determine quantities based on age. The most common recommendation is to subtract the age of the investor from the numbers 100 or 110. A person who is 25 years old will ideally allocate 75% - 85% of their funds to stocks, while only 15% - 25% is allocated to bonds. For a 60-year-old, the equation is revised so that 40% - 50% is invested in bonds, while 50% - 60% is invested in stocks.

Some investors like this rule and apply it to their investment portfolios. However, others find it too simplistic since it does not take into account investors' risk tolerance. Therefore, the best approach would be to use a combination of stocks and bonds in various industries. The best way to accomplish this is to focus on low-cost index funds. Many investors prefer to be safe rather than take significant risks. So they prefer to invest their money in low-cost index funds.

Essential factors for successful portfolio development

1. The return on investment: One of the most critical aspects of your investment

portfolio is its profitability. You should periodically monitor your finances, which are best accomplished using ROI or ROI. It is advisable to determine what has generated each dollar invested. There is a formula to calculate this figure.

ROI = (Benefits - Costs) / Costs

Even then, investors must understand that the return on investment depends on many other factors, such as the preferred type of investment security, etc. Also, keep in mind that a high ROI implies higher risk, while a lower figure means reduced risk. For this reason, proper risk management must be carried out.

2. How to measure risk: All investments carry an inherent risk. That's why investors and financial experts like to say that risk and reward are necessarily two sides of a coin. Investors should measure their level of risk tolerance, so they know what type of investments or assets to choose. For those looking to increase their investments by possibly double digits,

risky investments may promise higher returns. Investors looking to maintain or moderately grow their accounts may opt for less risky assets.

One of the most reliable ways to mitigate risk is to select stocks with extreme care. This is because some are considered safe, while others are considered risky. As an example, penny stocks may not necessarily enrich you, but they are more hazardous than other options. On the other hand, government bonds do not pay much, but they are very reliable and pose little if any, risk. Yields are almost guaranteed, but quantities are low.

In general, investment risks come mainly from the level of volatility. Volatility can cause the price of an asset to skyrocket or collapse. That is why it is much better to diversify investments in a portfolio. This helps minimize risks and stabilize the entire investment.

Also, remember that precious metals like silver and gold generally work well when the market is in recession. The same is true for technology stocks that tend to rise when markets are trending upward. Such information is crucial for investors, especially those who do not have access to professional advice.

Diversification of portfolios

Sometimes there is a risk of over diversifying. This means that even if diversification is an excellent approach to invest, it shouldn't be overdone. The main objective of diversification is to level out the valleys and peaks caused by regular market fluctuations and manage long-term market downtrends. Investors should avoid adding something to their portfolios that have the potential to backfire.

In summary

Investors should, at all costs, avoid risking their investments. Many investments are highly risky. These represent a high risk to a portfolio and can quickly eliminate any gains made by other more successful assets. Better to leave speculative investments alone.

Therefore, when planning a portfolio, an investor should keep his goals in mind at all times. Try and identify the asset classes that will help you meet your investment objectives, not those that are too risky or too passive.

Also, an investor's risk tolerance should be assessed. Younger investors trying to grow their accounts and generate wealth can take on riskier companies. However, older investors looking to manage their wealth should opt for safer investments, such as government bonds, as they are considered extremely safe.

Investors should also focus their energies on sectors in which they have some form of basic understanding. For example, a software engineer may want to look at technology stocks, while a banker may do well to invest in financial stocks. This way, you will have a reliable intuition regarding the performance of stocks within your sector. People lose money when they invest in industries of which they have little or no understanding.

Finally, it is essential to know when to get rid of stocks. Selling the shares at the right time means that investors get the best possible price. Too often, some tend to hold onto their stocks and are unwilling to let it go.

Knowing when to sell is crucial to a successful investment.

Chapter 13: The Main Tools Used In

Day Trading

Ever come across this saying that a day trader is only as fine as the tools they are working with? In this chapter, we shall take a look at the different tools used in day trading.

Best Software for Day Trading.

A day trading software is a term given to any software that can help in the decision making and analysis in order to make a trade. Some of the software will provide you with accessibility to the tools and all the resources needed.

A day trading software has the following basic features:

Any software should have the functionality of allowing the set up of trading strategy in the system.

Possess the order-placing function which is normally automated.

Tools for continuous assessment of the market developments so as to act on them.

How does trading software works?

Day trading software can be divided into four different categories:

Charting. Bright day traders will normally chart their prices using different charting software. However, some outside vendors normally offer feeds with charting packages which help in the analysis of technical indicators. Most of these data feeds are normally advanced packages.

Data. Before any day trader begins trading, you should be aware of the prices of the stocks, its future, and current currencies.

Execution of trade. After sourcing for the data and analyzed it on a chart, at some point, a day trader will need to enter into trade. Trade execution requires some sort of trading software. A good number of trading software nowadays allow you to develop your own trading strategies using APIs (Application Programming Interface). Some even specifically provide trading capabilities that are automated for day training.

Below are some of the platforms for day trading you can select.

Zacks Trade.

Zacks Trade is a brokerage day trading platform mostly for the US and international consumers. It started its trading since 2014 and its offices are suited in Chicago.

This online platform is mostly for active traders and investors. Investors on this trading platform need to make a deposit of around $2500 for them to register an account with the broker. However, if you are seeking help to make a trade, Zacks is the best choice for you since it offers brokerage trades for free. The tradable securities involved on this platform include market stocks, exchange-traded funds, and bonds. On this platform, you can make market trades more than 91 exchanges in different countries.

The cost per share of the commission is around $0.01 with a minimum of $3. This platform is mostly preferred to the active and options traders, investors seeking to trade on foreign stock exchanges and also those who want to access a human broker.

Zacks Trade offers two types of accounts; Zacks Trade Pro normally for the active users and Zacks Trader for the retail traders. Zacks Trader has a simple user interface, therefore, making it easy for the users to navigate through the system.

The pros of this software are that:

☐It is quite rare to find a trading platform that offers cheap commission such as a cent. To engage in trading the penny stocks, you will need to pay around 1% of the trade's value with a minimum cost of $3. The cost for options is around $3 for the first contract and cost of additional ones which is 75 cents.

☐Zacks normally offers investors with the accessibility to 26 research and 87 reports on subscriptions.

☐This software is also available for Linux users. Account-holders can also access Zacks using their mobile phones unlike it is seen on other software.

☐Zacks Trade is so safe and secure. Clients normally have their own platforms from the management and they register for their accounts with unique usernames and passwords.

☐Good customer service. This platform enables day traders who use their smartphones to trade for a free 24/7 hour basis. It is mostly for traders suited in Asia, the US, and Australia.

The shortcoming for this software is that it offers slightly higher charges on shares as compared to Interactive brokers.

Interactive Brokers.

This software is strongly advisable for advanced and frequent traders. It charges $0.01 per share with no minimum investment required. It offers a wide range of investments such as European bonds for the government and the corporate. Interactive brokers offer research for free to its traders from around 100 providers such as Zacks and many more.

The advantages of this software include:

☐ The low commission charges on exchange-traded funds and stock tend to favor the frequent traders. The low rates also favor the margin traders.

☐Interactive Broker's workstation is fast and offers great features such as watchlists, real-time monitoring, and advanced charting.

☐Another great advantage of Interactive Broker is that it offers its traders massive accessibility to research and news services which keeps them up to date.

The greatest shortcoming of Interactive Brokers is that traders find it hard to navigate through the website. This makes it difficult for traders to identify the costs associated with the commissions and fees.

TD Ameritrade.

This is one of the largest trading brokerage software with the basic and Thinkorswim platforms. It charges fees of $6.95 per share and no minimum investment is required. The Thinkorswim platform allows clients to customize color schemes and layouts according to their choice of preference. Trade tickets are found on both of the platforms so a trader can enter an order in whichever platform you are using.

After the software development team made updates on the tools and content of this software, there has been an improved look on both of the platforms making it more responsive to the client's devices.

TD Ameritrade offers a range of tradable securities; over 300 exchange-traded funds are free of charge and over 12,000 mutual funds. It also provides investors and traders accessibility to research for good quality trade execution especially for traders using the Thinkorswim platform.

The pros of TD Ameritrade include the following:

☐Offers wide news and research abilities to the traders which keep them up to date.

☐Provide a full range of investments such as forex and bitcoin futures trading for the right clients.

☐Provide massive education support for the traders. There are videos and also articles that provide simple guidelines to the traders on how to use the tools provided. It is so difficult to find a trader who cannot use this software despite you being a guru or a newbie.

☐ TD Ameritrade offers mock trading accounts. Traders are given virtual money of around $100,000 for practice. Traders can backtest trading strategies and access foreign futures.

The biggest shortcoming of TD Ameritrade is the high charges on commission and the exchange-traded funds as compared to other software.

TradeStation.

TradeStation is a day training software that charges $5 per share and requires a minimum investment of $500. It normally focuses on good quality data of the market and the trade executions. Its system is well established and normally remains firm during market surges. You can establish your own system using the analysis tools and mock testing strategies provided by this software.

The advantages of this software are as follows:

☐The platform has minimal chances of crashing down since it is a stable platform.

☐ The software feature out excellent charting tools and backtesting strategies making it the popular software.

☐Education support for this software is at top-notch. It normally offers classes and educational videos to its traders on various topics such as margins and many others.

The shortcoming of this software is that there no cases of forex trading and international trading is limited.

eOption

eOption is another day trading software that focuses on quality. It has a minimum investment of $500 and charges $3 per trade. The massive number of fans of eOption is mostly after the low commission and the extreme faster trade executions.

You can check out the platform before opening the account by using Paper Trading Toolset which is given for free for around 45 days.

This software has various pros:

☐It is easy for traders to navigate through the web-based platform. The user interface is so simple and the tools provided are easier to be found by the traders.

☐Good customer service. The platform is so stable and seldom has cases of crashing down.

☐The cost of using this software is very low since the charge per trade is $3. However, users for inactive accounts are normally charged an annual fee of $50.

The cons of this software are:

☐Limited accessibility for the traders to research and news providers unlike in other software.

☐Education support is not that good. The offerings are limited making it difficult for new traders.

Firstrade.

This is a trading software which is free of charge and requires a minimum investment of $0. It began offering $0 commission to traders dealing with options and the stock recently and for its benefit, it offered limited tools and research for the traders using this software. Firstrade also has this lending program which provides lending services to financial bodies and account holders and they can generate income. The traders can even sell the stock with no restrictions.

Some of the pros of this software include the following:

☐ It provides a set of accounts. It has simplified English, traditional and even Chinese accounts.

☐ It has lower costs. Charges $0 for the stock and options traders.

☐ This software provides access to stocks, options and funds type of trading.

The drawbacks of this software include the following:

☐ Firstrade does not provide access to forex, future and crypto type of trading.

☐ It does not have a 24/7 basis for customer support. They only operate in limited hours as compared to other brokerage trading platforms.

☐This platform has a few functionalities for its traders. Its traders are forced to use functionality from other platforms.

TradingView.

This is a trading software that is free, also has monthly charges of $9.95 for the Pro account, $19.95 for the Pro+ account and $39.95 for the premium account. Trading View does not support stock options and U.S trading.

A trader can make trades on the charts and the software will work out for you the profit and loss reports and analysis.

Its advantages include the following:

☐This software is of ease of use even to beginners.

☐Offer support for a variety of trades such as stock, forex, and cryptocurrency.

☐The charting for this software is easy to use and provides you with various tools.

The disadvantage of this software that turns many off is that it has no real-time news for the traders, unlike other trading software.

Tools and Services Used for Day Trading

For an effective job in day trading, a trader is required to possess a set of tools and services. Some of the tools required are the basic ones that you already possess such as a laptop or computer and a telephone.

Other tools that a trader may need include a charting platform and also real-time data. The tools and services needed by a day trader to be on the move include the following:

☐Laptop or computer.

Technology nowadays keeps on changing rapidly. A trader should at least possess a good laptop or computer with excellent memory and processors. A good computer processor will speed up the trade executions for excellent trade results. Also, a machine with high memory will have the capability of backing up the market data and there will be minimal chances of the computer crashing down.

☐Charting software.

Day trading software provided by companies or outside vendors normally have different features. Some software has charting platforms where traders can keep track of the price changes of the stock. Price charts make work easier for traders making their work effective and efficient. Software that lacks charting platforms makes it tough for new traders making contributing to slow trades. A day trader should mostly prefer software with charting platforms.

☐Internet.

Internet is one of the crucial resources required by online users. The Internet with fast speed produces effective work. A trader is able to be up-to-date with the current prices in the market. Workflow also becomes smooth since there is no lagging behind web pages unlike it is seen on slow internet. A trader should, of course, set high priorities for service providers with good internet speeds for excellent works.

☐Telephone.

In case you need to cut down the costs of the internet, a trader is advised to possess a cell phone or a landline. A telephone will assist you in contacting your broker in case your offline. You will need to back up the broker's contact number on your telephone for assistance.

☐Real-time market data.

Market data constitute of prices and markets you choose to trade. The market can be futures, options, forex, and even stocks. It is upon you as a trader to decide on the type of market you want and contacts your broker. Some brokers offer all the market data for free but with high commission.

☐Broker.

A day trading broker can be a company or small brokers. A broker provides a trader with the necessary market trades according to your choice of preference. Different brokers provide software with different features. Some may include platforms with all trades others with limited trades. Software with all trades most times requires payment of high commission ending up being a big burden for the inactive and small traders. It is mostly advisable to select smaller but regulated brokers who provide lower commissions.

Key Parameters in Day Trading

Despite the trading strategies, the key parameters in day trading to put into considerations are as follows:

☐Day trading volume.

This is a great day trading metric that helps traders identify the liquidity of an asset. High day trading volume help traders enter and go out of position so faster and easier.

169

☐Liquidity.

Liquidity is a crucial parameter for day traders who make profits from many trades. Traders normally monitor the trading volume of the market trade to determine its liquidity.

☐Price volatility.

This is essential for traders to monitor the price fluctuations in the market. Traders are able to monitor profits from prices that are short term.

Essential Tools Used for Day Trading

The a-must tools that a serious day trader need to have included the following:

☐Trading platform.

With the emergence of modern technology, online traders should possess online trading platforms. These platforms are normally provided by different companies and have different features. These platforms should be advanced and firm with no bugs. There is trading software available on smartphones and users can access anytime and anywhere. You should choose software that is cheaper and will not burden you.

☐Monitors.

Having access to multiple computer monitors is an added advantage to a day trader. Computer monitors help in keeping track of the performances of the stock, price fluctuations, news and also the key parameters. This promotes the effective performance of a day trader in the market.

☐News and data feed.

Possession of multiple computer monitors and an advanced trading platform will definitely keep the news and data feeds up to date. Out of date news feeds bring confusion and wrong information about the stock performance and prices in the market.

☐Research skills.

A trader needs to have marvelous research skills. The skills will help you understand the capital for the stocks market and the key parameters needed for day trading.

☐ Faster Internet.

High-speed internet is so crucial for any trader making a living with day trading. Such a kind of Internet makes work easier since trade executions become faster. Day traders normally require up-to-date news and data feeds and therefore slow-speed internet is so risky for online day traders.

☐ Capital.

Like any other kind of business, capital is a required necessity. Day traders need sufficient capital for the trading volume. This will enable traders to manage their volumes accordingly for better profits.

Chapter 14: Keys To Successful Day Trading

No-one can guarantee your day-trading success. It is a difficult business because, from the beginning, you are up against the brightest. From my own experience as well as from many successful traders I've coached, here are five key steps that, if followed earnestly, will put you on the right path to successful trading.

Bear in mind that this is not a "get rich fast" workaround for someone new to day trading. As with most things in life, you must apply yourself to be consistently successful. To become a professional trader, find the following three points:

Having discipline in any profession but particularly in stock trading, is of paramount importance. You will need to set some specific guidelines and rules as a day-trader to follow. It's quick to get off track if you don't have clear instructions to hold in any frameworks. Anything outside of those parameters could very likely throw off your focus and cause you to make an error that you would not typically be so inclined to make. Day trading is not the kind of business one should have the attitude of "shooting from the hip" or "letting the dices fall wherever they can." If you intend to achieve some kind of income or sales targets in trading, discipline is essential.

Find a day-trading or swinging trading strategy that works well for you, and practice on that strategy until you are professional. It is important to have several approaches so that you can manage various trades as they present themselves. This might apply to trade in stocks, forex, futures, ETF, or index trading.

Learning day-to-day trade requires one to apply oneself by studying the different trading concepts and studying strategies, of course. To have any kind of success, one has to be willing to put the time in. It may be tedious at first, but when you start growing up as a day trader and experience achieving your goals, the time you've committed to learning would be worthwhile. At the end of each trading day, do a practise of reviewing your trade. This is an excellent habit of studying and everyday practice. Study and make notes about your trades. Put these questions to yourself:

Have you ever found that there is more definite energy about people who have the right attitude? People with a negative attitude exude an energy that is very different or less alluring. Which one you'd prefer to be around most? While observing positive versus negative people, a positive attitude produces more success than a negative attitude is easy to see. So you say you want to make your day-trading career a success. There needs to be a good mindset instead!

From time to time, each has a hard day. Being a positive or a negative person doesn't stop you from having a bad day. So yeah, from time to time, you'll have a poor day in stock trading or another trading strategy of the day. It is the way you approach the rough day that will decide whether or not you can resolve it. Stay positive, and you are more likely to improve your trades!

Learn How to Read the Day Trading Map

Many in the trading sector are looking to sell the latest indicator or system to you. The claims are always high, not so much as the results. You get a buying signal that last week was successful, but this time, it's not. This happens very frequently. Why that failed is unclear.

The volume shows the fuel behind the market; the price of that fuel is the result. For example, when volume expands after a long rally, but the price does not rise, it could signal that the market has reached a peak. It shows you, at the very least, that sales are flowing into the rally. None of the indicators tells you that. During all phases of a market cycle, there are specific price and volume patterns and trade setups. Learning these trends will provide you with a true advantage in trade.

Master Day Trading with Handling Sound Money

There is no trading system at 100%. Trades would still lose out. Money management lets you decide how much to gamble on each deal, and even with a series of losses, keep you in the game. It will help to define position sizing and inform the level of the stoppage. Trading success will be elusive without sound money-management practices.

Money management is more than just figuring out how much you ought to risk on any particular trade. It also contains things such as when to step up a size. For example, if you're on a trend day, you know this market has high odds of closing at its extreme. This is the time when sound money management says it puts the maximum size of your position on. Such periods will make a big difference for the week or month in which you benefit.

Develop a Plan for Trade

For professional trading business, you need a business plan. The time to figure out how much to risk when you're about to enter a trade isn't enough. Creating a proposal would go without saying you follow your business strategy.

Grasp Day Trading's Mental Game

A lot is going on 'between the ears,' which is impacting your trade. Few traders put a lot of energy into the psychological side of trading before they lose out or realize their intuition is working against them-for instance, they can't pull the trigger on a sound trading setup. Many professional athletes focus on their game's mental side, as it gives them a competitive edge. One can say the same about trading. Learn to increase your chances of success on both sides.

Trade practice

Trading well depends on the development of specific competences. How can you develop ability without putting it into practice? For an aspiring trader, simulation and paper trading are highly valuable practices. Also, traders with experience will be learning a new concept of exchange.

Honored traders remain neutral; staying impartial means being emotionally removed from your decisions on trade. I met many day traders who, after losing $100 or even less, suffered emotionally for the rest of the day, and when they made $1000, they would be "on top of the world." They do not trade neutrally.

If you're like that, then your business will be driven by fear and covetousness; if you're down $100, you probably won't want to lose, just because you know you're going to suffer emotionally. If you're up to $1000, you may want more, even if you're supposed to take profits. Or you may end up taking profits prematurely because you're afraid the position might turn against you. Professionals don't let their account faze them with the day-to-day oscillations. One week's results matter little, not even the monthly results. For beginners, emotional ups and downs are very natural.

Staying neutral also means seeing the market changes as they actually are, not just how you want them to be. You can all know the situation a trade is going against you, so you're beginning to look for other explanations why it's still a successful trade, and you should be keeping it. That's very risky as it causes people to break their stops and lose big. You have to be absolutely clear about your entry and exit criteria before you make a trade. You can still find a justification to go up or down in your place, but you no longer see the actual price change.

Change from Prediction to Reaction

Under no conditions does a day trader attempt to predict future price changes. We have to play the actual price action as traders, not what we think the change will be! Please leave the forecast to investors. They mix investing and trading. That, too, is really risky. While there may be reasons to enter a position for a short-term trade, when it goes against them, they often end up holding it as an investment. Talk of Enron, always.

Yeah, there have been occasions where trade may have been acceptable during the Enron sell-off. Even for a short recovery, I held Enron from about $8.5 to $10 the problem is, if you base your entry on the belief that the company is cheap and that it needs to recover, you'll be more and more inclined to hold or even add to your position once it goes down. The stronger your opinion about a stock, the harder it is to make decisions based on the actual movement in prices.

I would strongly advise you to have a separate, basically based trades account.

You get too much leverage from a day trading account, making it very tempting to take risks that are far too high!! I'm not saying that expectations are not right; everyone should know what their future trades will most likely do. However, if those assumptions are incorrect, we must recognize that and respond to what is happening.

Conclusion

Trading is a tough endeavor to undertake but there's no need to complicate it needlessly. By following a structured approach, you too can realize the immense potential it has to improve your life. You might be wondering about exit opportunities and about how capital raising works?

Generally, I would advise beginners to not worry about this just yet. Once you have the results, capital will come. However, there is the danger of you risking far too much capital due to not realizing the amount of investment capital you can potentially raise. Everyone gets into trading for the money and freedom potential it provides in our lives so it is unwise to ignore it.

If you can follow strict risk limits and guidelines to an institutional level, you can have your trading account audited and use this as part of a job application to hedge funds or to proprietary trading firms (prop shops.) Truth be told, it won't be easy to land a trading position at a hedge fund but prop shops are more than accommodating of traders who have a good track record.

In addition to this, there are trading incubators, the most famous being Axiselect, which is run by the Australian broker Axitrader which helps traders transition over a three to five year period from a retail trading platform to an institutional level ("Trading Incubation Program", 2020). They will help you raise money and will shop your track record around for you so you don't need to worry about sinking your life savings into trading in order for you to make money.